Grow
Vegetables
in pots

LONDON, NEW YORK, MUNICH,
MELBOURNE, DELHI

Senior Editor Chauney Dunford
Project Editor Emma Callery
Project Art Editor Alison Shackleton
Managing Editor Penny Warren
Managing Art Editor Alison Donovan
Jacket Design Assistant Rosie Levine
Senior producer, Pre-production Tony Phipps
Producer, Pre-production George Nimmo
Senior Producer Seyhan Esen
Art Director Jane Bull
Publisher Mary Ling

DK Publishing
North American Consultant Delilah Smittle
Senior Editor Rebecca Warren

First American Edition, 2013

Published in the United States by DK Publishing,
375 Hudson Street, New York, New York 10014

13 14 15 16 17 10 9 8 7 6 5 4 3 2 1
001—192042—Jan/2013

Published in Great Britain by Dorling Kindersley Limited.

A catalog record for this book is available from the
Library of Congress.

ISBN 978-1-4654-0617-0

DK books are available at special discounts when
purchased in bulk for sales promotions, premiums, fund-
raising, or educational use. For details, contact: DK
Publishing Special Markets, 375 Hudson Street, New
York, New York 10014 or
SpecialSales@dk.com.

Printed and bound by South China Co. Ltd, China.

Discover more at
www.dk.com

Grow
Vegetables
in pots

Contents

GROWING VEGETABLES IN POTS

GROWING FRUIT IN POTS

PROBLEM SOLVER

EDIBLE INSPIRATIONS

Pots provide space to grow bumper crops of fruit, vegetables, and herbs, whatever your garden size or style. They also offer the opportunity to decorate your plot with stunning displays, the containers lending your growing space a unique style. This chapter is brimming with ideas to help you develop a productive container garden that will provide a feast for both your eyes and your plate.

You can grow your produce in any manner of container; group them together for a stunning and flexible display and savor the lush foliage, beautiful blossom, jewellike fruit, and fascinating roots and pods.

Productive pots for patios

Infuse a sunny patio with color, texture, and rich pickings by planting a range of crops in stylish pots. Devise creative ways to fill all the available space, thinking vertically as well as making use of any flat surface that is available. Something like an old stepladder could be useful, for example. Try trailing cherry tomatoes and strawberries from the steps, or allow beans or squashes to scramble up the ladder from large containers set at the base.

Space fillers

Pack your patio with a feast of productive plants. Valuable vertical space is often overlooked, but training soft fruit plants up fences and walls allows them to grow to their full size without invading your outdoor space. They look great, too. Citrus trees enjoy a sunny spot and bring a Mediterranean flavor to a summer patio. Growing citrus in containers is recommended because it allows you to move them indoors when fall arrives and return them to the patio in late spring after the last frost. Other fruit trees, including peaches and figs, also need a sunny situation, but are hardy enough to stay outside all year.

*Above: **Training fruit trees** along the wall of a patio is both attractive and fruitful. A sunny patio wall tends to be sheltered and warm, making it perfect for warmth-loving plants as long as you keep on watering.*

*Right: **A citrus tree** is always a most attractive plant, especially in the summer months when its fruits ripen, so is a particularly good choice of container plant for a patio. Bring it indoors in the winter, though.*

Make it varied

When planning what to grow in your containers, bear in mind that year-round pickings are invaluable. Mixed loose-leaf lettuce looks great springing from containers next to trailing nasturtiums and are ready to cut just six weeks after sowing. Try sowing seed every two or three weeks for salad leaves from spring to fall. Celery root will not mature until fall, but its large parsley-like foliage looks impressive as it grows. For winter interest, include evergreen herbs, such as aromatic rosemary, and hardy vegetables, like kale, both of which can be picked sparingly through the colder months. You may need to use every flat surface and container you can find to fulfill this diversity, but it will be well worth it.

Top: **This patio** is filled with a wide choice of salad leaves that are ready to eat now and vegetables that will be ready later in the year. Plan carefully and you can have crops on your patio year-round.

Above: **Grow salad crops in recycled drink cartons** or plastic tubs. These plants have shallow roots and are suitable for a wide range of containers as long as there are drainage holes in the bottom.

Productive pots for the garden

Containers can be used to add structure and style to your garden, as well as offering extra space for crops. Where existing soil conditions are poor or you want to grow something in a special medium, such as lemon or lime trees that grow best in an acidic citrus medium, pots can also provide the right growing conditions. Think about the color and shape of the edible contents as well as the containers themselves to ensure they give maximum impact.

Add some structure

Dot your fruit and vegetables among permanent plantings in a border or arrange them *en masse* for a spectacle that is definitely good enough to eat. With creative planning and planting, any garden can be both elegant and productive.

Fixing pots to the upright posts of a pergola, for example, is just one way of squeezing more plants into the garden. Strawberries are perfect for growing in elevated positions, where their clusters of scarlet berries will hang enticingly over the edge of the pot, making them easy to pick. At the same time, they will be more difficult for slugs and birds to reach than when the berries are growing in containers on the ground.

*Above: **A living sculpture** that is decorative as well as edible is always a great addition to the garden. For a change of pace, consider planting herbs such as parsley and thyme or a mixture of salad leaves in pots like these. Small containers dry out quickly, so make watering them a daily priority.*

*Right: **The importance** of the shape of containers can't be overestimated as they can so successfully add to the structural impact in the garden. Contemporary designs have their place and when filled with burgeoning crops, they make a particularly strong statement that is hard to overlook.*

Add a focal point

Crops set within a flower border provide a focal point while their colors and forms complement the adjacent ornamental plants. Silvery-blue kohlrabi leaves and bright variegated mint, for example, will stand out against the deep green foliage of surrounding shrubs. For even greater emphasis, choose brightly colored containers that also complement—or contrast with—the plants that are growing around them.

Scattering pots of fruit and vegetables in sunny spots between flowers has another particularly good advantage. They can make it more difficult for pests to locate the fruit and vegetables and yet help to attract pollinating insects where they are required for a good crop.

Above: **Blackberries** *grow happily in a large container resting in a perennial border. Both fruit and container add impact to their surroundings.*

Left: **Grouping containers** *of vegetables and herbs makes even greater impact in a border. A range of leaf color and form is visually stimulating as well as being tasty to eat.*

Compact crops

Containers brimming with vegetables, fruits, and herbs can supply color and convenient crops in a sunny space on a terrace, balcony, or windowsill. No space is ever too small for a container or two. If you are planting vertically, especially on a balcony or roof terrace, just ensure that the pots are carefully secured.

Small space planting

If you have a limited amount of space in which to grow your vegetables, herbs, and fruit, think creatively. Create a decorative screen perfect for a small courtyard or balcony with a row of towering string bean plants. Rustic wooden window boxes are simple to make, too, and you can tailor them to fit your window ledge. Line them with plastic, pierced at the base to provide drainage, and fill with a display of flowering herbs and salad leaves. A strip of copper around the container would add a decorative flourish and will also deter adventurous slugs and snails.

Above: **Compact,** *purple-flowered thyme, glowing golden marjoram, and lofty tarragon make good planting partners for a sunny sill. When they have finished flowering, cut them back to ensure healthy growth.*

Right: **Grow string beans** *in groups for good pollination and plant them in large, deep pots. Keep watering them thoroughly and they will provide a delicious crop of beans later in the summer months.*

Going up

Green wall systems are the ultimate space-saving crop containers and create a lush, vertical tapestry of foliage and fruits, perfect for any courtyard or terrace. Once planted, water and feed the crops by hand or you can install an irrigation system to do the job for you.

Up on a balcony, plant soft fruit in large stylish pots and choose a selection of strawberries and currants that will provide a long harvest throughout the summer and fall months. Currants are vigorous plants that make attractive specimens, and are also useful for creating low screens or enclosing private areas.

Above: **Strawberries** *grow well in confined but well-lit spaces. Black and red currants are also good choices. Scrambling stems of thornless blackberry cultivars look great trained on a trellis.*

Left: **Specially designed** *fabric pockets can be firmly attached to a framework on a wall. Fill them with medium and plant up with whatever crop—or crops—you like.*

Mini kitchen gardens

Planting a wide array of crops in raised beds and stylish pots makes any small space come alive with color and texture. Devise creative ways to use all the available space, and grow fruit and vegetables that can be cooked or eaten fresh from the plant. Don't feel that you have to restrict yourself to containers on the ground; fixing large galvanized containers to a wall, for example, will give your garden even greater versatility.

Use raised beds

Heat-loving crops will thrive in a raised bed set against a south-facing wall or fence. Plants like chiles, peppers, and eggplants, which may otherwise need the warmth of a greenhouse or windowsill indoors, will enjoy the conditions in a sunny bed. A brick wall provides the best backdrop, because it reflects extra heat during the day and releases stored heat at night, allowing exotic plants to thrive outside in cooler climates. They are also ideal for planting early summer crops and germinating many seeds because the medium in raised beds is relatively warm compared to the soil in the ground.

*Above: **Pack a sheltered raised bed** with a wide variety of salad leaves, zucchini, and peas. They will grow quickly and fruitfully as long as they are watered regularly.*

*Right: **A raised bed** needn't be the only container against a sunny wall. Stand smaller pots of other sun-loving vegetables, such as Swiss chard and tomato plants, in front to make the most of the location.*

Top: **Woven willow surrounds** *lend practical growing bags a decorative cottage-garden style, adding to the beauty of an informal patio when filled with crops and flowers.*

Above: **Smaller fabric growing bags** *can be dropped into any convenient hole or gap, such as between areas of paving, allowing you to make best use of the space available.*

Use fabric growing bags

Plastic-coated fabric growing bags make great raised beds and particularly suit small courtyards and patios where space is at a premium or fruit and vegetables are only grown in summer. They are tough, easy to move and store, and are available in a range of sizes, from 2ft (60cm) planters to substantial raised beds. Many bags have drainage holes made in them already, but it is essential to check for them before filling with medium.

Try planting leafy crops between towering sweet corn and climbing squashes or beans, or pack smaller beds with herbs and a range of colorful salad leaves. The bags are also deep enough to allow several tomato or pepper plants to be planted and produce good crops.

Crop and flower combinations

Beautiful plants in their own right, fruit and vegetables can be combined with ornamentals to create striking container displays. Choose a few edible flowers, too, for delicious blooming pots. Nasturtiums, pot marigolds (*Calendula*), and violas all have vibrant blooms that taste as good as they look, while herbs, including thyme, marjoram, and chives, have fragrant flowers as well as aromatic leaves.

Add bright color

Add welcome color to productive containers and raised beds with flowering herbs and annual bedding plants, such as verbenas and salvias. Both enjoy full sun and are planted afresh each year, so you can emphasize the changes alongside whichever crop you choose to plant. Verbenas and salvias are especially good options as their vivid colors complement both leafy and fruiting crops, and scented French marigolds (*Tagetes*) may even help to deter pests. Also try nasturtiums or other annual climbers in tandem with string beans for taller displays.

   Add winter interest to fruit pots, too, by smothering the soil beneath a blackberry or fig tree with the colorful foliage of evergreen heucheras.

Above: **French lavender** (Lavandula stoechas) *mirrors the form of the sweet corn plants behind, and also livens up the leafy potatoes, which can look a little dull on their own.*

Left: **Decorate a table** *with an edible meadow, using herbs, salad leaves, and tasty flowers. Here, the planter is sunk into the table, but the display would look equally appealing in a window box set on top.*

Keep it natural

Weave together fruit and blooms in rustic containers for a naturalistic look. Use alpine strawberries to make an informal edging, for example. Their white flowers and tiny ripening fruits will peep out from beneath taller vegetables planted behind and, unlike other forms of strawberry, they can tolerate the shade these plants cast. If growing larger fruit bushes and trees, which remain in their pots year after year, try partnering them with decorative perennials. For example, fill the gap between blossom time and ripe fruit by underplanting with a mist of blue catmint (*Nepeta*) or a carpet of pink *Geranium cinereum*.

Left: **The bright orange marigolds** *contrast delightfully with the bright red cherry tomatoes at the other end of the planter and add some zing to the herbs to the left and the peas and beans growing behind.*

Below: **An informal display** *of alpine strawberries, coreopsis, and pink impatiens introduce invaluable color to otherwise gray crates.*

Under cover crops

Seeds can be sown earlier and crops harvested later if you can find a space for them under cover, and even the smallest cold frame or a tiny greenhouse can vastly increase your productivity. In a greenhouse, intense summer sun can scorch the foliage of plants and raise the temperature far too high. To help, ensure there is adequate ventilation and put up shading in late spring and remove it in early fall. Blinds are expensive, but there are cheaper options.

Use hot spots

Even tiny greenhouses can be packed with crops, making the most of every inch of space. As well as pots of tomatoes, chiles, and eggplants, include a hanging basket or two planted with strawberries for an early crop.

Cold frames also protect crops against the cold and wet and are ideal for small spaces. Place them against a sunny wall or in a sheltered, light area, and use them for germinating seeds, hardening off young plants, and growing crops such as squashes that enjoy extra heat.

*Above: **To use a cold frame,** prop the lid open or remove it to provide ventilation during the day, and close or replace it at night.*

*Right: **In summer,** open the door and vents of your greenhouse in the morning to increase airflow, lower the temperature, and prevent a stagnant atmosphere from forming, which will only encourage diseases. Then close the greenhouse at night to retain heat.*

*Above: **Growing crops in crates** gives you plenty of options as they can be arranged to fit whatever space you have available. Line them up straight, or in staggered rows, as shown here.*

*Above: **Mini lean-to greenhouses** are perfect for protecting crops if you have limited space. They are very versatile with shelves that can be positioned at whatever height suits your crops at that particular time.*

Be creative

Make good use of space in a small greenhouse by setting your crops in staggered rows. Also keep tall plants, such as cucumbers, trained tidily onto their supports, with sufficient light and space around them to encourage the fruits to ripen. The space under staging can be used for pots of strawberries and herbs, if it's not too shady.

In a small garden, a mini lean-to greenhouse is an option, set against a sunny wall, or on a balcony or terrace. These small greenhouses range from models with a light metal framework covered with plastic designed to protect tomatoes in a growing bag, to more expensive and versatile glazed metal- or wooden-framed structures, with shelves to accommodate seed trays as well as taller plants.

Perfect partners

Combining pots and plants to create a balanced display is often a case of trial and error. Those with less experience may find it easier to opt for a collection of containers made from the same material, which will make a harmonious design for a formal or modern garden. A random group of pots in a variety of shapes, sizes, and materials is ideal for a cottage-style garden or an informal space. Either set your containers out in height order in a formal fashion, or in a looser way to produce a more relaxed display.

Matching materials

A uniform group of plants growing in pots made from the same material can be a highly effective way of creating a focal point on a patio or terrace. For contemporary gardens, choose containers in colors and a design or finish that echoes your interior decoration to create a seamless flow from inside to out, or throw caution to the wind and use pots that contrast with your décor to create colorful punctuation points.

Alternatively, set identical plants and containers in a row to divide or enclose a patio, or to frame a feature or gateway. Tall, elegant containers work particularly well in this context, especially if you choose materials that complement your garden style.

Above: **Match galvanized containers** *of varying heights and widths in a contemporary space to create a raised vegetable patch of chives, peppers, leeks, strawberries, and tomatoes.*

Right: **Confer a sense of unity** *on your garden design by placing similar containers throughout your space. This will help successfully draw the eye from one part of the garden to another.*

Mixing shapes and sizes

Groups of containers made from different materials, and in different shapes and sizes, are ideal for a relaxed space where a natural look is required. Add movement, scale, and a sense of perspective by grouping planters by height, or raise your game and create a collection on a table, bench, or even an old ladder, using the treads as a theater to show off the plants. Mixed pots tend to look unbalanced when arranged in a row, so try a more staggered display instead. Also include a few similar elements to unify your collection, such as pot and plant colors, foliage shapes, or a pebble mulch.

Above: **Same shape and finish,** *but different colors, unify this group of containers successfully. Eggplants and tomato plants also grow tall, so make a stunning feature when planted in such large pots.*

Above left: **For something a little more rustic** *look to willow baskets and galvaniszd tins. The containers may be a mixture of materials, but their overall casual country style makes them a pleasing entity.*

Left: **A casual group** *of colorful containers will instantly bring vitality to the corner of a patio or garden. By mixing colors, the effect is made still more striking, especially if you then plant thcm with colorful crops.*

PLANNING AHEAD

Growing your own fruit and vegetables in containers is easy, but working out where, when, and how to begin can be more challenging. It's also important to select the right containers and growing medium to maximize your plants' potential and get off to a flying start. This chapter covers this essential information, and also provides quick-reference seasonal planners for vegetables and fruit.

To get the most out of your crops, you need some basic equipment, know-how for planting seeds and potting on, and then how to continue caring for your crops once they are in their containers.

Planning crops in pots

Where space is limited, plan your crops carefully to achieve a long cropping season and a lush, colorful container display at all times of the year. From radishes and lettuce in the spring, to zucchini and tomatoes in the summer, and leeks and kale in the winter, you can ensure fresh produce on your table year-round. Selecting an appropriate site and a variety of crops that suit your needs, as well as having essential equipment on hand (*see pp.42–43*), will all help to ensure success.

Choose a site

One advantage of growing in pots is that they can be moved into the sun or shade, from indoors to outside, or from an exposed site to a sheltered one. Most productive plants require full sun for at least part of the day, but consider the needs of individual crops because while sunny spots are ideal for ripening fruit, they cause leafy plants to wilt and increase the need for watering. Wind can also desiccate medium, damage plants, and blow pots over, so avoid exposed sites if possible, or create some shelter around your crop display. Sunny windowsills, porches, and sunrooms are great places to grow crops throughout the year. For example, citrus trees fruit best in a cool spot indoors during the winter (move them outside in summer). Keep areas indoors well ventilated during the summer and protect young plants from intense light with shading or set them on a north- or east-facing windowsill.

Not all crops are reliant on full sun to thrive. If necessary, containers can be positioned in partial shade if your plants demand it.

Kohlrabi thrives in full sun. Seedlings are usually ready to harvest after six weeks when the bulbous bases are no bigger than a tennis ball.

Crops for all seasons

For a display that is perennially bountiful, grow a wide range of fruit and vegetables and be poised with young plants to replace those that are no longer productive. This is not difficult to achieve with a little planning and by growing some plants indoors or under cloches outside. Planning ahead is the key to success if you want a continuous crop over a long season.

First, decide what you would like to eat, and then find out when those plants can be sown and harvested. Also select a range of crops that will keep the garden full, and you and your family fed, throughout the year. Try to mix plants that crop over a long season, like zucchini, perennial herbs, and Swiss chard. Then combine these with quick-croppers such as radishes and salad leaves that mature in a matter of weeks, and can be sown every two weeks to fill gaps around any plants that may take longer to grow.

Citrus trees can be moved out into the garden during the summer months. They look wonderful nested in among other crops and plants.

PLANTS FOR SPRING

Most seed is sown in early spring, but any harvests at this time of year will be from overwintered crops like purple-sprouting broccoli. By late spring, however, sweet new-season treats, such as lettuce and beets, will be ready to eat. In spring, you can harvest:

Rosemary *p.131*

Radishes *p.84*

Peas *p.106*

Lettuce *p.76*

Rhubarb *p.148*

Beet *p.113*

Swiss chard *p.96*

PLANTS FOR SUMMER

Soft fruits and young vegetables are ripe for picking in the summer. The summer is also the time to sow some fast-growing crops every few weeks or so to crop at regular intervals and provide a continuous harvest. In summer you can harvest:

Basil *p.129*

Strawberries *p.152*

Potatoes *p.108*

Zucchini *p.91*

Tomatoes *p.86*

Blueberries *p.156*

String beans *p.100*

PLANTS FOR FALL AND WINTER

Fall brings a bounty of fruit and vegetables, many of which can be stored for leaner times. Winter crops can be enjoyed from the first frosts right up until late spring. In fall and winter you can harvest any of these tasty delights:

Chiles and peppers *p.92*

Apples *p.138*

Pears *p.140*

Potatoes *p.108*

Leeks *p.118*

Kale *p.98*

Witloof chicory *p.82*

Choosing and buying seeds and plants

Growing vegetables used to mean raising them from seed, but garden centers and mail-order companies now also offer a wide range of seedlings and young plants. Deciding what to buy is a question of how much time, money, and space you have, and which crops you choose to grow.

Seeds

Growing plants from seed is easy and immensely satisfying. Seeds are available from garden centres and mail-order companies, or collect them from plants that have been left to flower. Seeds offer the widest choice of vegetable cultivars, with options of size, habit, color, and disease resistance. Potatoes are grown from tubers, known as seed potatoes, while miniature onion and shallot bulbs, called "sets," provide an alternative to seed.

Crop choices All vegetables, but particularly root crops, are best grown from seed. Alpine strawberries are the only fruit worth sowing.
Pros Seeds are cheap, and a packet stored in cool, dry conditions can last several seasons. They also offer control over plant numbers and flexibility to sow little and often.
Cons Seeds take time, require small pots or trays, and need space, especially tender crops that are sown indoors.

Plug plants

These small plants are grown in modules and can be bought in garden centers or through mail-order seed companies. They are a useful option where space is limited or conditions are not suitable for raising plants from seed and they offer good value for money. However, such small plants are delicate and will need potting up and watering as soon as you receive them, especially if they have arrived in the mail.

Crop choices No fruit but most vegetables are available as plugs, particularly those that are grown in quantity, such as salads and leafy crops like Swiss chard.
Pros Quicker than sowing seed, plugs save time and space, and are economical, even for lots of plants.
Cons The range of cultivars available is more limited than for seed. Plants need careful handling, potting on, and acclimatizing to new conditions to avoid losses.

Planting your own seeds is always satisfying. Make sure your containers are clean and keep everything moist and warm.

Many different vegetables are available as plug plants. They will need potting on and watering promptly after you have bought them.

If you don't have the space to plant seeds indoors and pot them on, then young plants are a good alternative. Buy them after the last frost.

Young plants

Available from garden centers and mail-order companies, sturdy young plants grown individually in small pots offer gardeners the chance to try crops that may be too time-consuming or difficult to grow from seed. If there is only space for one summer squash, or a single specimen of several tomato cultivars, then buying them as young plants makes sense. Look for strong, healthy plants that look stocky, bright green, and well-watered. Carefully knock plants from their containers to check that the roots are not cramped and pot-bound, and plant out as soon as they are hardened off and conditions are suitable.

Crop choices Good choices include strawberries and rhubarb, as well as a range of fruiting vegetables, such as tomatoes, peppers, chiles, cucumbers, and eggplants.
Pros Larger plants make an instant impact and save the time and space needed to raise seedlings. They are valuable for heat-loving crops if you have nowhere indoors to sow and grow them on, and can be purchased after the frosts when they can be planted outside. They're also a good idea if you only need one or two plants.
Cons This is an expensive way to grow vegetables, and there is a much more limited range of cultivars on offer. Plants must be acclimatized to outdoor conditions, too, so don't buy too early if your indoor space is limited.

Trees and shrubs

Most fruit grows on trees and shrubs, which can either be bought growing in containers or as field-grown "bare-root" plants, which are lifted and sold when dormant between early winter and early spring. This dormant season is also the best time to plant fruit trees and bushes, although pot-grown types can be planted throughout the year. Container-grown fruit is widely available, while bare-root plants are usually only available from specialty fruit nurseries via mail order. Always buy certified disease-free plants and check that trees are growing on a suitable rootstock for pots (see pp.54–55). If you are buying single specimens make sure they are self-fertile; if they aren't self-fertile, you will need a suitable pollination partner as well.

Crop choices All fruit trees and bushes are available in these forms. Choose mature specimens that are ready to fruit if you want instant impact.
Pros Bare-root plants are cheaper and offer a wider range of cultivars on dwarfing rootstocks.
Cons Bare-root plants are only delivered in winter and early spring and must be planted immediately. Container-grown trees tend to be more expensive, with fewer cultivars on offer. Old stock can also be pot-bound.

Container-grown trees can be planted year-round, are widely available, and don't need planting immediately.

Container choices

Pots can add style to a plot or be purely functional, but they must hold enough medium to supply plants with sufficient water and nutrients, and have adequate drainage. For the best results, select containers that suit your style of garden and your choice of crops.

Choosing your pot

Terra-cotta and glazed pots flatter many fruit and vegetable plants. Terra-cotta is porous, and draws moisture from medium, drying it out quickly, while glazed pots stay moist longer. Their weight is also useful for anchoring taller plants but they can be difficult to move, so plant them in situ.

Plastic and man-made materials are durable, generally inexpensive, and perfect for most cropping plants. Reuse containers that plants arrive in and drill drainage holes in the bottom of trugs, buckets, and tubs. The material's light weight is ideal for containers that need to be moved, but not for exposed sites. Plastic pots also hold moisture well and need watering less frequently.

Metal pots make a stylish display and are practical too. As well as specially designed galvanized steel pots, you could improvise planters from old watering cans and large food cans, but always clean them very thoroughly. Most metals are long-lasting and retain water well, but they also heat up quickly. This is an advantage for tender crops,

Galvanized steel, with its resistance to corrosion, is a good choice for growing all manner of crops over many seasons.

but if you are growing salad greens that prefer cool conditions, line pots with bubble wrap before planting, as this will help conserve moisture throughout the summer.

Wooden containers and baskets bring a more rustic note to a productive display or add formality, depending on the style of the container. Large half-barrels, for example, provide plenty of space for crops, while elegant Versailles tubs suit the formality of pruned fruit trees.

Woven materials are light and make beautiful hanging baskets, but they are not very durable. Wooden pots and baskets may need to be lined; if a plastic liner is already in place, pierce it before you plant it up to provide drainage.

Plastic containers are available in a range of colors and sizes.

Old crates and wine boxes look good overflowing with plants.

Look for terra-cotta pots with frost-proof guarantees, but line them with bubble wrap before planting up for added protection during the winter.

Zucchini are greedy feeders so need plenty of depth in which to grow. It is best to plant them in a large container for the best results.

Choosing the size and style

Size matters when it comes to what's best for plants. In general, bigger is better. Larger containers hold more medium, and thus more moisture and nutrients, than smaller ones, making plants easier to look after. Herbs, such as thyme and marjoram, tolerate dry conditions and suit smaller pots, as do some fast-growing crops, like salad leaves. Nutrient-hungry tomatoes, zucchinis, and squashes perform best in large pots, and deep containers are essential for root crops, such as carrots and potatoes.

Containers come in a range of styles that can all be exploited. Mangers and growing tables are raised planters that are a comfortable height for sowing and planting. Large hanging baskets and deep window boxes are ideal for trailing tomatoes and herbs. Growing bags can be used conventionally or cut in half to create two containers, and made more decorative with willow screens.

Fruit trees will be at their best in large pots filled with specialized citrus or soil-based medium, designed to give them just the right nutrients.

Choosing the right potting medium

There are many mediums on the market and choosing the right one can seem complicated, but the decision is largely between soil-based and multipurpose types. Some multipurpose mediums contain peat, but environmental concerns about peat extraction has led to substitutes, such as coir-based medium.

Medium choices

There are three basic kinds of potting medium and the choices are outlined here. Multipurpose is fine for potting on plants in tubs and baskets, but for longer displays look for a medium mix that is suitable for its purpose. Be aware that cheap products usually mean poorer quality.

LOAM-BASED MEDIUM

Also called soil-based medium, this is made from sterilized loam, including the popular John Innes-style mediums. They're available in different recipes or strengths, and range from No 1 for seeds and cuttings to No 3, which contains the most fertilizer, for long-term large plants such as shrubs. Start feeding pot plants after three months when the nutrients run out.

PEAT-BASED MEDIUM

Also known as loamless or soilless medium, peat-based medium includes multipurpose types for general potting and mixes for seed-sowing. It is lightweight and well aerated, and the lack of nutrients is overcome by the use of slow-release fertilizers.

When you put medium *into pots, firm it down lightly with your hand before sowing seeds (see pp.44–45) or potting on (see pp.48–49).*

LOAM-BASED MEDIUM

Advantages
- The John Innes range is formulated for different types of plants
- Holds water well
- Contains good supply of nutrients

Disadvantages
- Bags are heavy
- Incorporates small quantities of peat
- Quality can vary so stick with a reputable brand

PEAT-BASED MEDIUM

Advantages
- Easy to handle, being light and clean
- Consistent, reliable quality

Disadvantages
- Dries out quickly and becomes difficult to rewet
- Low nutrient levels
- Plants need feeding after 4–6 weeks
- Not reliable for long-term displays

PEAT-FREE MEDIUM

As concern about peat-stripped areas and ruined habitats grows, so the sales of peat-free medium have increased. Traditional soil-based potting mediums are not completely peat-free, but they contain less than peat-based medium.

One of the best peat-free mediums is coir, as long as it is from a good source. Made from shredded coconut husks, coir contains no nutrients and is usually added to other mediums for use in pot-grown annual displays. The least environmentally damaging medium is compost-based medium. Made from recycled household waste and often sold by local government, it is suitable for most garden and container uses. Wood fiber, which commonly consists of stripped bark, pulverized wood, sawdust, or even paper waste is also used to make lightweight, free draining, peat-free medium that is ideal for plants in pots.

A downside of using peat-free mediums is that they can be very variable between brands and the blends of materials used. While all are suitable for growing plants, gardeners need to become familiar with their individual properties and characteristics to get the best results.

Choose the right medium and your seeds, seedlings, and more mature plants will thrive and provide you with plenty of produce over the months.

COIR-BASED MEDIUM

Advantages

- Similar to peat in terms of weight and moisture-holding capacity
- Lightweight and easy to handle
- It is particularly good for seedlings

Disadvantages

- Not for permanent displays
- Environmental credentials compromised because of the distance it is shipped

COMPOST- AND WOOD-BASED POTTING MEDIUM

Advantages

- Widely available and made from sustainable sources
- Wood fiber is easy to handle, being light and clean

Disadvantages

- Not for permanent displays
- May need to be mixed with other materials to improve its performance for particular plants
- Don't over water as can look dry on the surface when wet beneath

Preparing your pots for planting

All pots, large and small, need a few minutes to prepare before they can be used. Plants will live longer and look better if their pots are prepared well, so it is always worth spending some time on this. Also consider the weight of your containers and how best to move them to avoid back-breaking lifting after planting.

Making drainage holes

Most plant pots are made with drainage holes so that excess water can drain away (if it can't, plants will rot). If a pot doesn't have holes, however, you will need to make some. One way of doing this is to drill into the base several times with a masonry bit.

You can either leave the drilled holes as they are, or tap them with a hammer to make one larger drainage hole. If you are planning on growing sizeable plants, such as a fruit tree or bush, a larger hole would be preferable. Choose clay containers with a thick base, which is less likely to fracture when hit with a hammer.

Use a masonry bit *to drill small holes for drainage. For a larger hole, drill them close together and then tap them out with a hammer.*

Stopping the rot

To help water drain freely, place broken terra-cotta pots (crocks), polystyrene chips, or large pebbles in the bottom of the pot. Alternatively, use a layer of fine mesh with gravel on top. This prevents drainage holes from becoming blocked and medium being flushed out.

Old and chipped terra-cotta pots *can be usefully recycled. Break them into crocks and use them to help water drain freely from a container.*

TOP TIP: LIGHTENING THE LOAD

Any pot is heavy when filled with medium, and even heavier after being watered. The best way to lighten the load (although you may prefer not to do this for taller plants as they may topple over), is to fill the bottom of the pot with polystyrene chunks or ceramic balls.

Lining pots

Clay pots that have not been glazed on the inside are vulnerable to frost damage (*see p.71*). To prevent this, line pots that you want to leave outside all year with heavy-duty plastic and/or bubble wrap. Push it well down into the pot, and use a pair of scissors to cut out drainage holes in the bottom or simply leave the bottom uncovered. Add a layer of pebbles or stones, then fill up with medium, the weight of which will push the liner down further. Finally, trim away the excess liner flush with the top of the container. Lining terra-cotta pots in this way also prevents salts in the medium and water from leaching through the clay and discoloring your container.

Reusing old pots

All pots, including those left in the garden or stacked up in the potting shed or greenhouse, must be cleaned before use. The same goes for plastic seed trays that you are reusing. This applies even if the pots and trays were stored under cover and cleaned months ago, before being put away. They can be breeding grounds for pests and diseases, larvae, and baby slugs. Don't risk it.

Scrub the containers scrupulously with detergent and rinse well. As an extra precaution, you can also soak pots in baby bottle sterilizing solution and then rinse them well. This is especially advisable if the containers have previously housed diseased plants.

Bubble wrap is the perfect material to use when lining a ceramic pot to protect it from frost. Roughly trim the top before filling with medium.

A heavy duty scrubbing brush is ideal for cleaning old pots. Ensure you thoroughly scrub the outside as well as the inside of the containers.

Moving heavy containers

To avoid back injury, never lift filled, heavy pots. Place them in their intended site, held slightly off the ground on pot feet (*see p.71*) or small stones, before filling with medium and planting up. If this is not possible, place the empty pot on a small, sturdy wooden trolley, treated with wood preservative. Once filled and planted up, the pot can be moved safely.

The trolley can double as a pot stand, allowing water to drain away efficiently and protecting the pot from frost. Large stones placed next to the wheels will prevent movement and disguise them.

Stand a heavy container on a small wooden trolley before planting it up. You can then move it easily and safely without fear of hurting your back.

Caring for your containers

All containers need a thorough wash every so often to make sure they are clean and pest-free—but wood, metal, and stone pots may benefit from a little additional care to keep them looking their best. Make this an annual event to ensure they stay in tip-top condition for many years.

Protecting wood

To prevent wooden containers from rotting, avoid exposing any part of the container to wet medium. Treat it before use by applying a nontoxic wood preservative both inside and out. Repeat this treatment every year in winter, after you have cleaned out the container.

Alternatively, protect wooden containers with a nontoxic wood stain that contains preservatives. Make sure the timber is clean and dry before applying the stain. Bear in mind the colors of your plants when choosing the paint color to avoid alarming clashes. Quiet colors are invariably best because they blend with other pastels, and will set off brasher, bolder designs. Finally, protect the inner surfaces of a container by lining it with plastic, ensuring there are plenty of drainage holes in the bottom.

When protecting wooden containers with a preservative, choose one that isn't toxic to plants, such as linseed oil, and apply it with a soft cloth.

Preventing metal from rusting

Since galvanized steel resists rust, and stainless steel is unlikely to do so, rust isn't usually a problem. A metal watering can, left outside for several years, will still be rust-free. But if you need to drill extra drainage holes in a container, the drilling action may break through the protective seal, and rust may set in. To prevent this happening, apply an anti-rust treatment around and inside the drilled holes. In general, try to avoid scratching metal containers, and keep them clean using any general-purpose nonabrasive household cleaner and a soft cloth.

Use a nontoxic proprietary anti-rust treatment and follow the manufacturer's instructions when applying it to your metal containers.

Preparing clay pots

If terra-cotta pots have been put in storage over winter, before you use them again give them a good scrub in warm water and detergent to get them scrupulously clean, and then hose them down. Also, clean the pots at the end of the season before you put them away. Ornamental pots can be left out all year if they are frost-proof, but note that there is a difference between being frost-proof and frost-resistant: after a couple of winters outside, frost-resistant containers may start flaking and deteriorating. If in doubt, check with the manufacturer.

Before planting up clay pots, soak them in a bucket of water. This saturates the porous clay so it draws less water out of the medium.

Keep your reused containers clean and your fruits, vegetables, and herbs are less likely to be troubled by pests and diseases.

Aging stone containers

Modern or reproduction stone containers (or statues) often defeat their purpose by looking too clean, too bright, and too new when they're used to add instant antiquity. The quickest way to age a new stone pot is to promote the growth of algae by smearing it with a mixture of cow manure and water, rubbing it with grass, or painting the container with natural live yogurt. Some manufacturers of stone pots and ornaments make their own special aging solutions, which are quick and easy to apply with a clean paintbrush.

Among the ways to naturally age a new stone container is to encourage algae to grow (see above) by rubbing a handful of grass on the surface.

TOP TIP: KEEPING SYNTHETICS CLEAN

Like terra-cotta pots, synthetic containers should be cleaned and scrubbed in warm water and detergent before they are stored, and again when they are brought out for use. Remove stubborn stains with a scouring pad, but test a small, discreet area first to ensure that this will not scratch the pot. Choose a dark-colored container that won't show the dirt from permanent plantings that will sit outside all year.

Vegetable crop planner

Use this table to check when to sow, plant, and harvest your vegetables. Timings will vary for different climates, so adjust them for your own site and weather conditions. For continuity, replace crops harvested in spring and summer with plants sown later.

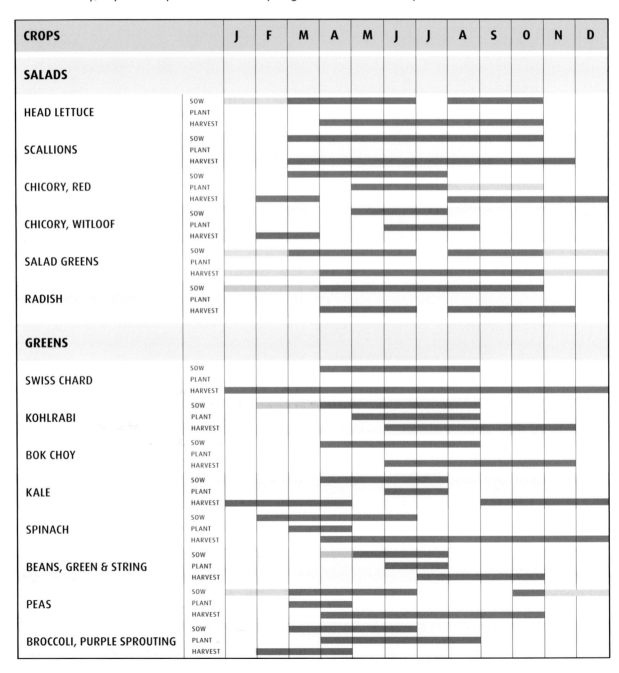

CROPS		J	F	M	A	M	J	J	A	S	O	N	D
SALADS													
HEAD LETTUCE	SOW / PLANT / HARVEST												
SCALLIONS	SOW / PLANT / HARVEST												
CHICORY, RED	SOW / PLANT / HARVEST												
CHICORY, WITLOOF	SOW / PLANT / HARVEST												
SALAD GREENS	SOW / PLANT / HARVEST												
RADISH	SOW / PLANT / HARVEST												
GREENS													
SWISS CHARD	SOW / PLANT / HARVEST												
KOHLRABI	SOW / PLANT / HARVEST												
BOK CHOY	SOW / PLANT / HARVEST												
KALE	SOW / PLANT / HARVEST												
SPINACH	SOW / PLANT / HARVEST												
BEANS, GREEN & STRING	SOW / PLANT / HARVEST												
PEAS	SOW / PLANT / HARVEST												
BROCCOLI, PURPLE SPROUTING	SOW / PLANT / HARVEST												

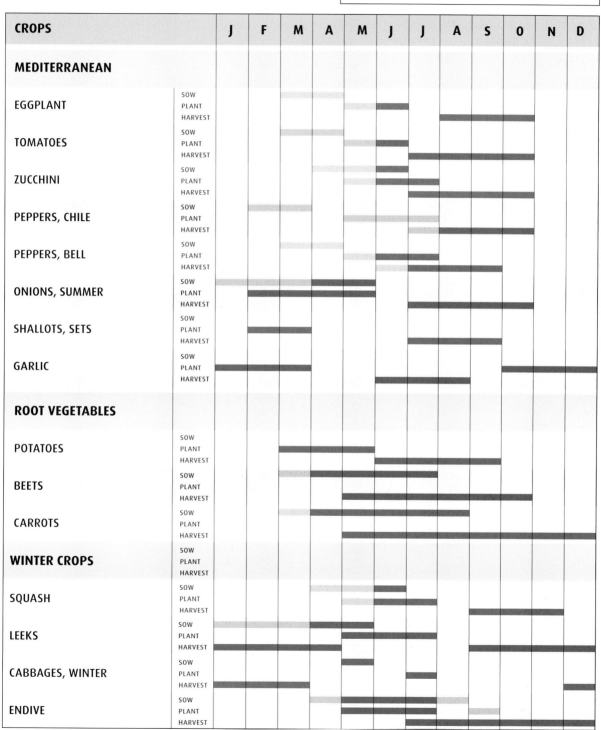

KEY	
	SOWN, PLANTED, HARVESTED UNDER COVER
	SOWN, PLANTED, HARVESTED OUTDOORS

CROPS		J	F	M	A	M	J	J	A	S	O	N	D

MEDITERRANEAN

EGGPLANT — SOW / PLANT / HARVEST

TOMATOES — SOW / PLANT / HARVEST

ZUCCHINI — SOW / PLANT / HARVEST

PEPPERS, CHILE — SOW / PLANT / HARVEST

PEPPERS, BELL — SOW / PLANT / HARVEST

ONIONS, SUMMER — SOW / PLANT / HARVEST

SHALLOTS, SETS — SOW / PLANT / HARVEST

GARLIC — SOW / PLANT / HARVEST

ROOT VEGETABLES

POTATOES — SOW / PLANT / HARVEST

BEETS — SOW / PLANT / HARVEST

CARROTS — SOW / PLANT / HARVEST

WINTER CROPS

SQUASH — SOW / PLANT / HARVEST

LEEKS — SOW / PLANT / HARVEST

CABBAGES, WINTER — SOW / PLANT / HARVEST

ENDIVE — SOW / PLANT / HARVEST

Fruit crop planner

Use this table to check when to plant, prune, and harvest your fruit. Timings vary for different climates so adjust them for your own weather conditions. Planting times refer to bare-root plants; container-grown shrubs and trees can be planted year-round.

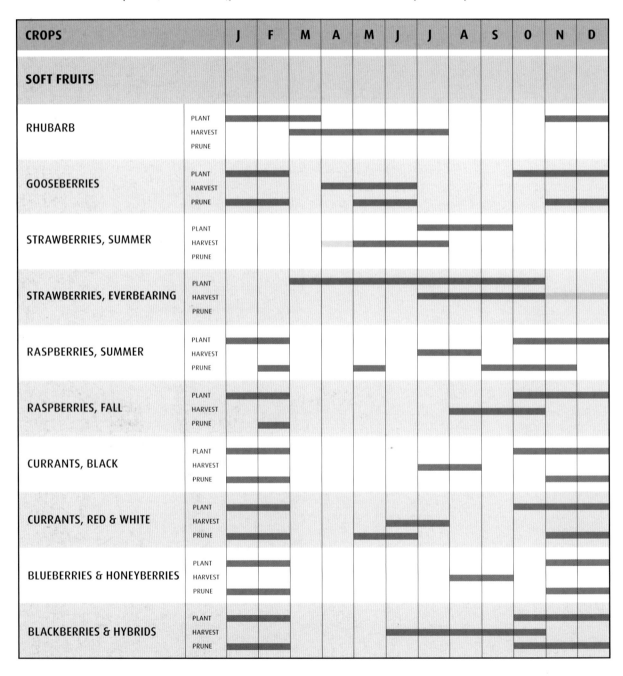

CROPS		J	F	M	A	M	J	J	A	S	O	N	D
SOFT FRUITS													
RHUBARB	PLANT												
	HARVEST												
	PRUNE												
GOOSEBERRIES	PLANT												
	HARVEST												
	PRUNE												
STRAWBERRIES, SUMMER	PLANT												
	HARVEST												
	PRUNE												
STRAWBERRIES, EVERBEARING	PLANT												
	HARVEST												
	PRUNE												
RASPBERRIES, SUMMER	PLANT												
	HARVEST												
	PRUNE												
RASPBERRIES, FALL	PLANT												
	HARVEST												
	PRUNE												
CURRANTS, BLACK	PLANT												
	HARVEST												
	PRUNE												
CURRANTS, RED & WHITE	PLANT												
	HARVEST												
	PRUNE												
BLUEBERRIES & HONEYBERRIES	PLANT												
	HARVEST												
	PRUNE												
BLACKBERRIES & HYBRIDS	PLANT												
	HARVEST												
	PRUNE												

KEY		
	SOWN, PLANTED, HARVESTED UNDER COVER	
	SOWN, PLANTED, HARVESTED OUTDOORS	

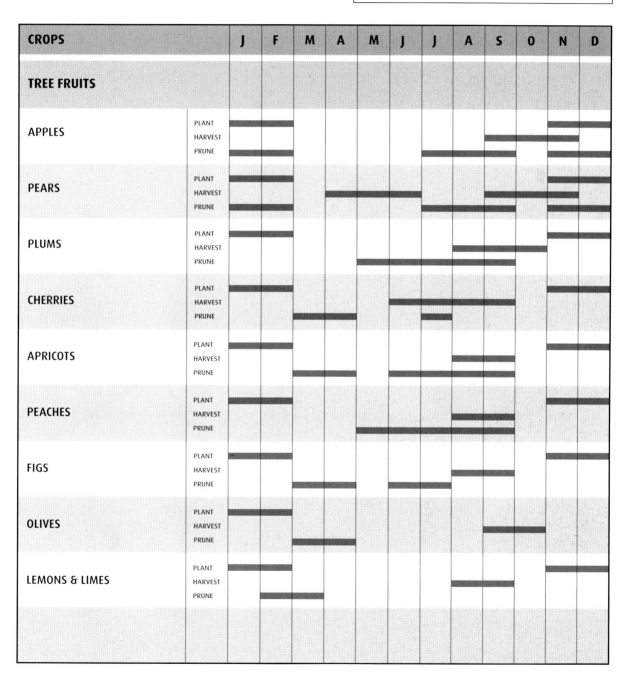

TREE FRUITS

CROPS		J	F	M	A	M	J	J	A	S	O	N	D
APPLES	PLANT	■	■									■	■
	HARVEST									■	■	■	
	PRUNE	■	■					■	■	■		■	
PEARS	PLANT	■	■									■	■
	HARVEST				■	■	■	■		■	■	■	
	PRUNE	■	■					■	■	■		■	
PLUMS	PLANT	■	■									■	
	HARVEST								░	░			
	PRUNE					■	■						
CHERRIES	PLANT	■	■									■	■
	HARVEST						■	■					
	PRUNE			■	■			■					
APRICOTS	PLANT	■										■	
	HARVEST								░				
	PRUNE			■	■								
PEACHES	PLANT	■	■									■	■
	HARVEST								░	░			
	PRUNE					■	■						
FIGS	PLANT	■										■	■
	HARVEST			■					░	░			
	PRUNE			■	■								
OLIVES	PLANT	■	■										
	HARVEST									■	■		
	PRUNE			■	■								
LEMONS & LIMES	PLANT	■	■									■	■
	HARVEST								■	■			
	PRUNE		■	■									

GARDENING KNOW-HOW

This chapter starts off by explaining which essential tools and equipment you need and then moves on to sowing seeds, potting on, and replanting. Followed by information on pruning more mature plants and protecting your crops from frost, it is packed with step-by-step sequences to help you on your way to growing healthy and fruitful crops all year-round.

The pleasure that is to be had from growing your own vegetables from seed can't be overestimated and some practical advice for growing the healthiest and most productive crops always helps.

Essential tools

Having the right tools and equipment on hand makes growing your own produce so much more straightforward. Most are things that you will use elsewhere in the garden, making them a worthwhile investment. Start with the essentials, and build up your tool kit over time.

Tools for maintaining your crops

The tools you need to grow fruit and vegetables are fairly basic; even if you're new to gardening, you probably own several of them already. When buying tools, choose the best quality you can afford—a well-maintained second-hand tool may last longer than a cheaper new one—and keep them in good shape so they will last for years to come. Gather them together after use, wipe them clean and store them in a dry place, such as a shed or garage.

Seed and cell packs These are useful when raising your own vegetable plants from seed. They tend to be fragile, and may only last a few seasons, but they are cheap to replace.

Hand fork and trowel Both are useful for planting out, harvesting, and for tending to containers. Use a small fork for weeding between plants, perhaps with a long handle.

Dibble These are useful for sowing large seeds individually, such as beans, or for transplanting young seedlings. They can also be used to plant bulbs, like shallot sets.

Pruners These are used to prune fruit trees and bushes, and should be kept sharp and clean. They are also used to harvest larger fruit and vegetables, such as winter squashes.

Tools for protecting your crops

Once your crops are growing in their pots there are a few extra tools that will help you keep them at their most productive. If you don't have a trug (*see right*), a bucket or plastic box can be very useful for storing the smaller items or for carrying them from container to container.

Canes and string Canes and branches are essential to provide support for tall, climbing, or weaker plants. Use raffia or soft garden string to then tie tender stems to the supports.

Cloches Over winter, bell-shaped glass or plastic cloches are useful to protect plants that aren't fully hardy. They are then used in spring for warming the soil and growing seeds.

Floating row cover This nonwoven fabric is ideal for protecting young and tender plants against frost, or for draping over spring-flowering fruit trees when frosts are predicted.

Netting Protect your fruit and vegetable crops against insect and bird attack using fine- and medium-grade netting. Carefully roll it up after use to keep it tangle-free.

Hand sprayers Keep these handy for spraying water on string bean and tomato flowers to improve pollination, to spray pesticides, or to increase humidity around indoor crops.

Pruning saw A sharp pruning saw is the best tool for successfully pruning larger branches of fruit trees. It can also be used for ornamental trees and shrubs. Clean the blade after use.

Sowing seeds in trays

Sowing small seeds in trays is a good idea because they are easy to clean and fit neatly into propagators or on bright windowsills. If you are reusing seed trays, clean them with hot water and detergent and then rinse them thoroughly before planting up. Most vegetables seeds are sown in this way, but always refer to the seed packet for instructions.

1 Fill clean seed trays with multipurpose or seed medium, and then use a second tray to firm it down. Lay the clean one over the medium, and press down gently and evenly across the surface.

2 Scatter seeds evenly over the medium, straight from the packet or from the palm of your hand. Sow thinly to prevent waste and overcrowding, which results in spindly seedlings prone to diseases.

3 Lightly cover the seeds with sieved medium and label the tray with the plant name and date. Water with tap water using a fine spray; avoid stored rainwater, which can cause damping-off disease.

4 Place the tray in a propagator or cover it with clear plastic to create warmth and humidity. Keep in a light place, such as on a windowsill, but not in strong sun. Remove the cover as soon as seedlings emerge.

5 When the seedlings have a few leaves, they are ready to transplant. Water them, then hold a seed leaf and loosen the roots with a dibble or pencil to gently tease each one from the medium.

6 Fill module trays or small pots with multipurpose medium. Water them and allow to to drain. Dibble a hole in each module, insert a seedling, and gently firm using the dibble. Water in and label.

After a few weeks you will have lots of seedlings growing steadily
that will soon be ready for potting again (see pp.48–49).

Sowing seeds in pots and outdoors

Sowing seeds in small pots works well for larger seeds and where fewer plants are required. Sow tender crops, such as tomatoes and zucchini, in small pots and let them germinate and grow indoors to start them off, but for seeds like beets, green beans, and lettuce, you can sow them directly into their containers outdoors *(see top tip, below).*

1 Lightly crumble multipurpose or seed compost into each pot until full. Firm it down gently and then push the seeds in to the correct planting depth, as described on the back of the seed packet.

2 Cover the seeds with a small amount of medium, water, and then put them in a propagator or cover with clear plastic until they germinate. Keep moist and thin the seedlings to leave a single plant in each pot.

3 Remove the seedlings from the propagator or leave uncovered and put them in a sunny spot, but out of direct sun. Pot them on as they grow *(see p.48)* to prevent the plants becoming root-bound.

TOP TIP: SOWING SEEDS DIRECTLY OUTDOORS

1 Fill your container to within 2in (5cm) of the rim with an equal mix of multipurpose and soil-based composts. Sow seeds as specified on the packet. Water and place in a sheltered spot.

2 When the seedlings have produced four leaves or more, remove the weakest to allow the others sufficient space to develop. Check the seed packet for spacing; you can usually grow plants a little closer in pots.

3 Keep the seedlings well watered; if they dry out, their growth will be inhibited. At the other extreme, you must also safeguard against waterlogging, so stand seed pots on "feet" or pebbles.

Grow tender crops on under cover until frosts have passed and plants can be planted out. Pot indoor crops into their final containers once they are large enough and the weather is warm enough (see pp.52–53).

Potting on

It is vital to pot on plants as they grow to prevent the roots from becoming pot-bound, resulting in the plants failing to thrive due to lack of space and nutrition. Then, as the risk of night frosts lessen in late spring, you can harden them off prior to planting them out in containers *(see pp.52–53).*

1 When roots appear through the base of the pots, it is time to repot the plants individually into larger containers. Pot on gradually to ever larger pots, filling them each time with multipurpose medium.

2 Root disturbance checks growth so keep the root ball intact when potting on plants and handle them gently. Feed regularly with a balanced liquid fertilizer to encourage healthy growth.

3 Harden plants off gradually in a cold frame or place them outside during the day and bring them in at night. Plant them out into large pots before the roots become restricted, and water in well.

TOP TIP: GROWING BAGS

For crops that are nutrient hungry, such as tomatoes and eggplants, pot them on into growing bags. To conserve moisture, make the planting holes just large enough to plant into, but leave some room so you can water easily.

To acclimatize the seedlings *to outdoor conditions, harden them off in a cold frame with a lid that can be easily opened by day and closed by night.*

Sowing seeds directly into pots

With some crops, such as micro greens and watercress, you can sow the seeds into a pot, allow them to grow indoors, and then harvest directly from their container without having to pick out and pot on. Sow batches of seeds at regular intervals for a summer-long supply and keep the pots in a light and warm place, but out of the way of direct sunlight. Turn them regularly.

1 Use growing bags or fill pots or seed trays with medium. Sow the seed according to the spacings given on the packet. Some salad leaves are sown deeper or more thickly than others.

2 Keep the seed bed moist until the seeds emerge in a week or so. Pick leaves individually as soon as they are large enough to use. The plants will continue growing and produce more.

3 Harvesting the plants checks their growth and they will take a week or two to recover. Water them well to promote regrowth. Expect two or three similar harvests before the plants run out of steam.

TOP TIP: GROW WATERCRESS FROM SEEDS AND CUTTINGS

1 Watercress is hardy but can be started under cover. Fill pots with medium, firm gently and water well. Sow seeds thinly on the surface, cover lightly with medium or vermiculite, and water.

2 Keep the pots on a bright windowsill or in a warm greenhouse, standing in saucers of water, 2in (5cm) deep. Keep the medium moist at all times. Thin the seedlings to leave the strongest.

3 Once the risk of frost has passed, move the pots and trays outside. Keep them topped up with water. To take cuttings, stand stems in water and leave on a windowsill. Once roots develop, pot up.

The method of sowing seeds in trays described opposite (top), also suits cut-and-come-again
salad leaves. Feed them with a high-nitrogen liquid fertilizer to encourage a large crop.

Planting a container

When planting young crops like this Swiss chard, ensure that your containers have holes at the bottom for good drainage, and that plants are well-spaced and firmed in. It is important to have suitable gaps between each plant for maximum yield. Plant them too close together and they will be fighting for sun and nutrition.

1 Prepare your container as described on pp.32–33, adding plastic liner if you are using a terra-cotta pot. Then fill the pot with multipurpose medium up to 2in (5cm) from the top, firming it down as you work.

2 Set the plants out in the pot while they are still in their containers to see how many you need and if the spacing between them is adequate. Water the plants before knocking them out of their pots.

3 Make holes in the medium with the correct distance between each plant (4in (10cm) for Swiss chard). Place a plant in each hole to the same depth it had in its previous pot. Firm the medium around it.

4 Water the plants thoroughly, using a sprinkler on a watering can, to settle the medium around the plants' roots. Continue to water the container regularly, particularly during hot weather.

Plant vegetables and fruit in variously sized containers, tailoring them to the amount of space
the plants will need to grow. Mixtures of vegetables can add interest to large containers

Planting a fruit tree in a container

Given the right care, many fruit trees flourish in containers and produce generous crops. Choose a young two- or three-year-old tree grafted onto dwarfing rootstocks, such as virus-certified for apples or Pixy for plums and apricots. Very dwarfing rootstocks, such as M27 for apples, are not so successful when restricted to pots. Select a self-fertile variety or grow another fruit tree nearby to promote pollination.

1 Apples, pears, plums, cherries, figs, peaches, nectarines, and apricots all thrive in pots. Before planting your chosen fruit tree, however, thoroughly soak the tree's roots in a bucket of water.

2 Buy a large container at least 20in (50cm) in diameter and with drainage holes in the bottom. Place broken pottery, stones, or polystyrene chunks in the bottom to prevent soil from clogging up the holes.

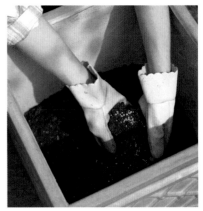

3 Add a deep layer of soil-based medium, such as all-purpose potting soil, to the bottom of the container and mix in some slow-release fertilizer granules, according to the rate specified on the packaging.

4 Leave the tree soaking until bubbles stop rising to the surface of the water. Lift out to drain; remove the pot, and tease out the roots. Stand the tree in its new container, ensuring the stem is upright.

5 Be sure that when the tree is planted its root ball will sit at the same depth as it was in its pot. Fill in around the roots with medium mixed with slow-release fertilizer, firming it with your fingers as you go.

TOP TIP: PEACH TREES

A dwarf peach cultivar is ideal for growing in a pot. In winter, bring into a cool place near a window to protect against frost and reduce the risk of peach leaf curl (see p.182). Dust the flowers with a soft brush to aid pollination.

Feed annually in spring *by carefully removing the top layer of medium and replacing it with fresh medium mixed with a slow-release, granular fertilizer. Keep the medium moist at all times.*

Repotting a fruit tree

All fruit trees need occasional repotting to give their roots space to grow and to provide them with fresh, nutrient-rich medium. Move trees in the process of growing into a larger container every year; mature specimens need repotting every couple of years, but the pot can remain the same size. It is best to do this in late fall, although any time from winter until early spring will do.

1 Gently knock the plant from its existing pot. Larger trees may need to be laid down on the ground carefully and pulled by the trunk; ask someone to help you if the pot and root ball are heavy.

2 Holding the trunk, carefully tease out the roots around the edge of the root ball. Trim the roots using pruners. Select long, thick roots and any that have been damaged. Make a clean angled cut.

3 Choose a new pot for the tree (for size, see above) and be sure that it has drainage holes. Use fresh, soil-based medium and plant at the same depth as it was before. Firm and water well.

TOP TIP: REPOTTING A FRUIT BUSH

1 Given large pots, fruit bushes grow into substantial shrubs that need little pruning. Prepare a 15in (38cm) pot (see pp.32–33), add compost, and stand the bush's pot at the same level as before.

2 Remove the plastic pot and carefully place the plant into the remaining hole. Firm around the root ball to remove any gaps, and dress the top of the pot with a little more suitable medium.

3 Place the pot in sun and cover with netting to prevent birds eating the berries. A cane teepee frame with netting stretched over it is secure, but easy to remove and replace when picking fruit.

Repotting is best done *at any time from late fall until early spring, weather permitting, while the fruit trees are dormant.*

Caring for container plants

Plants in hanging baskets, pots, and planters require more hands-on care than those grown in the ground, where their roots have greater access to soil moisture and nutrients. Plants confined to containers require you to supply all their water and food needs, but there are some useful tips that you can follow to make these jobs a little easier and to save time.

Fruit trees and bushes that will live in their pots for a few years benefit from an annual application of all-purpose fertilizer in spring.

Tomato fertilizers are a good choice for any flowering or fruiting plants. Follow the manufacturer's application instructions on the label.

Feeding plants

There are three basic nutrients that plants require to maintain good health. These are nitrogen (N), which is needed for leaf and shoot growth; phosphorus (P), required for good root development; and potassium (K), which helps flowers and fruits to form. All-purpose fertilizers usually contain a balance of all three nutrients, but those that are formulated to promote good fruit or flower production will have a high potassium content, while fertilizers for leafy crops or foliage plants contain high levels of nitrogen.

CHOOSING FERTILIZERS

Granular fertilizers labeled "slow-release" or "controlled" are best, as these are easy to apply and will continue to feed plants over the whole growing season. If you want to boost flower or fruit production, give your plants additional doses of a liquid tomato fertilizer as soon as the flowers start to form. If you are growing plants with specific needs, such as citrus trees, buy a fertilizer formulated for that particular plant.

TOP TIP: MULCHING

Spreading a thick layer of material, known as a "mulch," on the medium's surface looks attractive, helps to retain moisture, and prevents weed seeds from germinating. Options include leaf mold and bark chips; gravel and slate provide a decorative touch. Apply a layer of mulch at least 1in (2.5cm) deep after watering the medium.

Watering

Keeping thirsty plants supplied with water is essential if you want to maintain their health and vigor throughout the summer. Small terra-cotta pots need watering the most frequently, while tall containers made from plastic or other man-made materials will require slightly less attention. Covering the medium with a layer of mulch will also help to seal in moisture (*see the top tip, opposite*).

When planting up your containers, ensure that you leave a gap of 2in (5cm) between the top of the medium and the rim of the pot to allow space for a layer of mulch and water to accumulate and filter down to the plants' roots. To prevent scorching your crop's leaves, water early or late in the day, and aim your watering can or hose onto the medium, where it's needed, rather than the leaves.

Above: **A good soaking** *once or twice a week, so the water reaches the bottom of the pot, is more effective than a daily light sprinkling.*

Left: **If you don't have time** *to do lots of watering, choose large pots, which hold more medium and therefore larger volumes of water.*

Automatic irrigation

If you work long hours, are going on vacation, or have lots of patio containers to look after, consider installing an automatic watering system. Most systems come in kit form, consisting of a timer, which you attach to an outside faucet (there are also kits available to fit rainwater barrels), and a network of tubes into which you insert feeder pipes and small drip nozzles that deliver water directly to your pots.

Some systems are a little fussy to install and you will need to read the instructions carefully. If you are finding it difficult to attach the feeder pipes or drip nozzles, soak the tubes in hot water for a few minutes to soften the plastic. Also, check your plants every few days to ensure that they are not being over- or under-watered and adjust the flow or watering period accordingly.

Top left: **Run a main pipe** *alongside your containers and attach a feeder pipe at the necessary point with a connector for each container.*

Top: **Attach drip nozzles** *to the feeder pipes and lay them on the surface of the medium.*

Left: **Fit the timer** *on the faucet, and set it to water in early morning or in the evening when it is cooler and evaporation rates are low.*

Pruning raspberries

Summer-fruiting raspberries flower and fruit on stems (canes) that grew during the previous season. These varieties often produce taller stems than fall types, so need support against a "ladder" of horizontal wires. Fall raspberries fruit for a longer period than summer types, often producing berries until the first frost. Because of their fruiting habit, the plants may crop in their first season (*see also pp.158–159*).

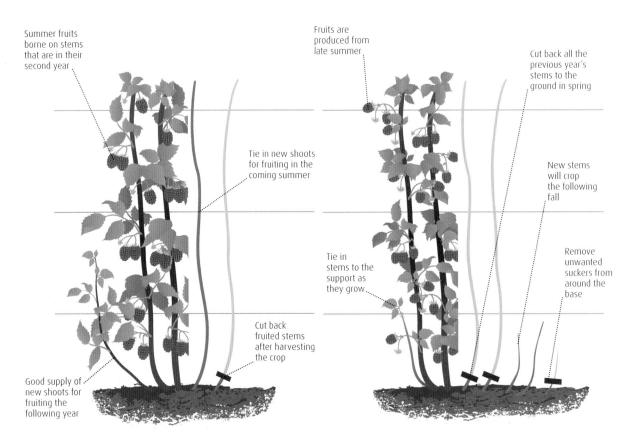

Summer fruits borne on stems that are in their second year

Fruits are produced from late summer

Cut back all the previous year's stems to the ground in spring

Tie in new shoots for fruiting in the coming summer

New stems will crop the following fall

Tie in stems to the support as they grow

Remove unwanted suckers from around the base

Cut back fruited stems after harvesting the crop

Good supply of new shoots for fruiting the following year

Summer raspberries

For formative pruning, shorten all the canes immediately after planting. For established pruning, cut only the fruited canes back to ground level after harvesting the crop. They do best in a sheltered spot in cool areas and annual pruning will help to keep the canes productive.

Fall raspberries

For formative pruning, cut all stems to the base the first winter after planting. New shoots will appear from below the soil in early spring. For established pruning, cut all growth down to ground level annually in spring. Dig out unwanted suckers from around the base of the plants.

Pruning blackberries

Blackberries and related hybrid berries produce a plentiful supply of large juicy fruit (*see also pp.150–151*). Plants are best trained on horizontal wires. The shoots that develop in the first year will not fruit until the following year. As they grow, weave them into the wires, pulling them as close to horizontal as possible. The following year, allow new canes to grow upright, tying them loosely to the upper wires.

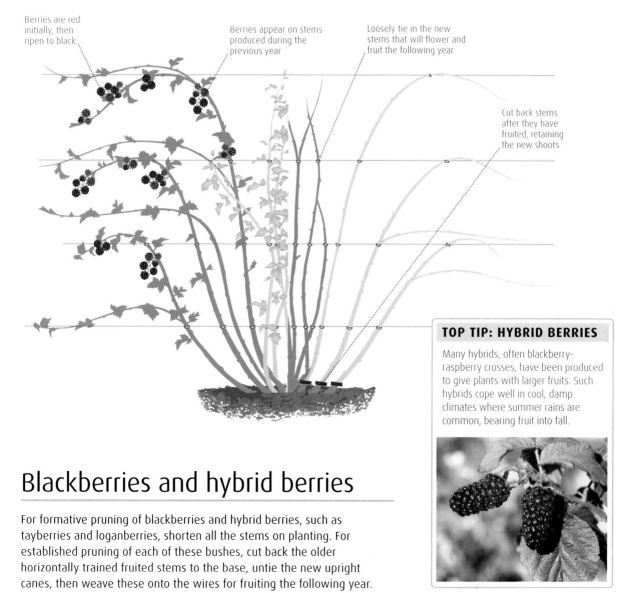

Berries are red initially, then ripen to black

Berries appear on stems produced during the previous year

Loosely tie in the new stems that will flower and fruit the following year

Cut back stems after they have fruited, retaining the new shoots

TOP TIP: HYBRID BERRIES

Many hybrids, often blackberry-raspberry crosses, have been produced to give plants with larger fruits. Such hybrids cope well in cool, damp climates where summer rains are common, bearing fruit into fall.

Blackberries and hybrid berries

For formative pruning of blackberries and hybrid berries, such as tayberries and loganberries, shorten all the stems on planting. For established pruning of each of these bushes, cut back the older horizontally trained fruited stems to the base, untie the new upright canes, then weave these onto the wires for fruiting the following year.

Pruning currants

Black currants are neat-growing, twiggy, deciduous shrubs that benefit from annual pruning. For red and white currants, prune a young plant to three or four strong stems on a short trunk. Allow shoots to develop without pruning in spring and summer—initially, they will not flower or fruit. The following winter, reduce these to eight to ten main branches. The shoots that emerge from this main framework will carry the crop (*see also pp.146–147*).

Black currants

For formative pruning, cut back all stems down to within 4in (10cm) of the base. Growth in the first year will not fruit. Prune to create an open-centered bush—the unpruned stems will flower and fruit the following year. For established pruning, cut out up to one-third of the older stems annually to encourage new growth.

TOP TIP: PRUNING OTHER CURRANTS

Start by shortening strong stems by up to half. Once established, cut back the previous year's fruited sideshoots to one bud from the base and remove unproductive branches.

Well-spaced branches with an open habit

Cut out one-third of the older fruited stems

Ripe fruits hang down in long clusters

Once the bush is established, remove any twiggy growth that will not fruit

Pruning gooseberries and blueberries

Gooseberries crop most heavily if spurs from the main branches are kept stubby. Blueberries, however, flower on the previous season's wood. Strong shoots that appear between spring and summer will bear fruit the following year, so do not prune them (*see also pp.149 and 156–157*).

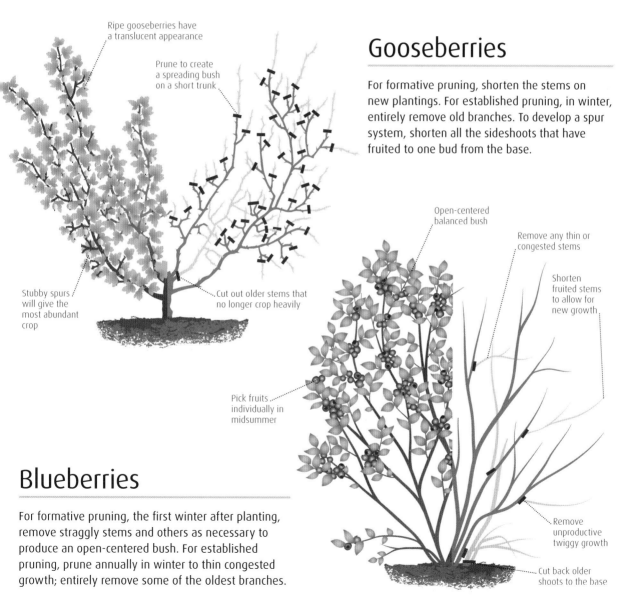

Ripe gooseberries have a translucent appearance

Prune to create a spreading bush on a short trunk

Stubby spurs will give the most abundant crop

Cut out older stems that no longer crop heavily

Gooseberries

For formative pruning, shorten the stems on new plantings. For established pruning, in winter, entirely remove old branches. To develop a spur system, shorten all the sideshoots that have fruited to one bud from the base.

Open-centered balanced bush

Remove any thin or congested stems

Shorten fruited stems to allow for new growth

Pick fruits individually in midsummer

Remove unproductive twiggy growth

Cut back older shoots to the base

Blueberries

For formative pruning, the first winter after planting, remove straggly stems and others as necessary to produce an open-centered bush. For established pruning, prune annually in winter to thin congested growth; entirely remove some of the oldest branches.

Pruning apples and pears

Apples and pears are best grown on dwarfing rootstocks. Some apples carry their fruit at the ends of stems produced the previous year ("tip-bearing" trees), but most plants are "spur-bearing," holding their fruit on short sideshoots. On tip-bearers, cut back a few of the older stems each year. On spur-bearers, shorten all new growth up to one-half. Cut back weaker shoots hard and remove unwanted shoots at the base (*see also pp.138–139*).

Apples

For formative pruning, train free-standing plants in containers as half-standards or bushes. For established pruning, prune mainly in winter. Go gently. Hard pruning of mature branches results in unproductive, whippy shoots.

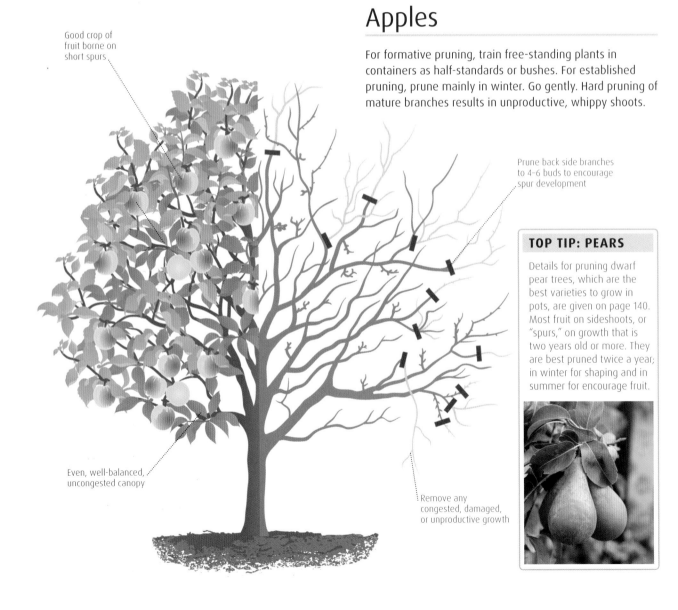

Good crop of fruit borne on short spurs

Prune back side branches to 4-6 buds to encourage spur development

Even, well-balanced, uncongested canopy

Remove any congested, damaged, or unproductive growth

TOP TIP: PEARS

Details for pruning dwarf pear trees, which are the best varieties to grow in pots, are given on page 140. Most fruit on sideshoots, or "spurs," on growth that is two years old or more. They are best pruned twice a year; in winter for shaping and in summer for encourage fruit.

Pruning cherries

Sweet and sour cherries have different pruning requirements, so ensure you know which variety you are growing. Sweet cherries fruit on wood that is two years old or more, so pruning thereafter should be minimal. Sour cherries, on the other hand, fruit only on one-year-old stems, so prune accordingly. To reduce the risk of infection, prune cherries in warm, dry spells in spring to early summer (*see also p.142*).

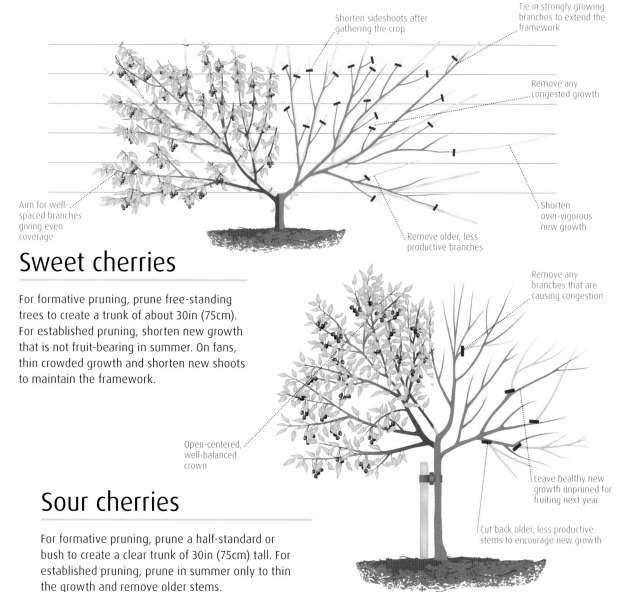

Shorten sideshoots after gathering the crop

Tie in strongly growing branches to extend the framework

Remove any congested growth

Aim for well-spaced branches giving even coverage

Shorten over-vigorous new growth

Remove older, less productive branches

Remove any branches that are causing congestion

Open-centered, well-balanced crown

Leave healthy new growth unpruned for fruiting next year

Cut back older, less productive stems to encourage new growth

Sweet cherries

For formative pruning, prune free-standing trees to create a trunk of about 30in (75cm). For established pruning, shorten new growth that is not fruit-bearing in summer. On fans, thin crowded growth and shorten new shoots to maintain the framework.

Sour cherries

For formative pruning, prune a half-standard or bush to create a clear trunk of 30in (75cm) tall. For established pruning, prune in summer only to thin the growth and remove older stems.

Pruning plums and peaches

All pruning for these fruit trees should be done during warm, dry periods in summer to minimize the risk of infection. Thin the fruit, if necessary, removing any that touch, will touch when ripe, or that are not exposed to the sun, as these may not ripen properly. On wall-trained peaches, shorten any new growth that shades the fruit and then, after harvesting, cut back the fruited branches and tie in replacements (*see also pp.143 and 160*).

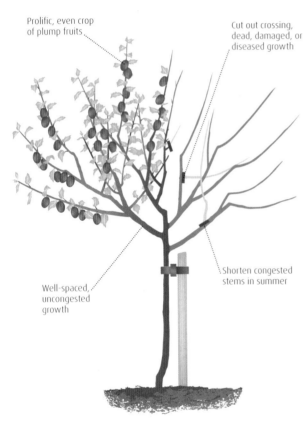

Prolific, even crop of plump fruits

Cut out crossing, dead, damaged, or diseased growth

Well-spaced, uncongested growth

Shorten congested stems in summer

Plums

For formative pruning, grow free-standing plants as a tree or bush or train on wires as a fan. For established pruning, thin growth as necessary in summer and reduce the number of plums. On fans, remove older stems and tie in replacements. Shorten shoots after harvest.

Peaches

For formative pruning, train free-standing plants as a fan with an open crown of up to ten main branches. For established pruning, prune in summer to thin the growth and reduce the number of peaches. Cut back fruited stems on fans and tie in replacements.

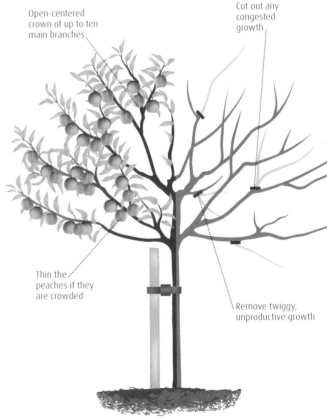

Open-centered crown of up to ten main branches

Cut out any congested growth

Thin the peaches if they are crowded

Remove twiggy, unproductive growth

Pruning apricots

Pruning and training of young apricot trees are best done in spring. For a bush or tree, aim to retain three or four main branches with an open center on a clear trunk at least 30in (75cm) tall. If necessary, thin the fruit in early summer. On established fans, remove any leafy growth that shades the developing apricots in summer. After harvesting, cut back the fruited branches and tie in replacements (*see also p.161*).

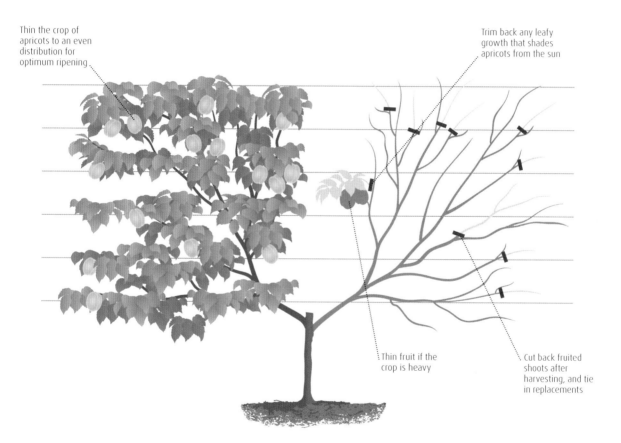

Thin the crop of apricots to an even distribution for optimum ripening

Trim back any leafy growth that shades apricots from the sun

Thin fruit if the crop is heavy

Cut back fruited shoots after harvesting, and tie in replacements

Apricots

For formative pruning, prune free-standing plants with 3–4 main branches; train fans on wire supports. For established pruning, prune in summer to remove unproductive growth and to thin and expose ripening fruit. On fans, cut back fruited shoots to suitable replacements and tie in to the wire supports.

TOP TIP: GROW AS A FAN

Apricot trees are more likely to ripen in a cooler climate if they are grown against a south-facing wall, which reflects heat. Fan-train an even framework of branches, tied to horizontal wires.

Pruning figs and olives

In warm climates, fig trees produce two or three crops annually; in cool climates, only one crop will ripen fully, so production must be carefully managed. Tiny figs that develop toward the end of the growing season will overwinter and ripen the next year, so remove any undeveloped or unripened figs in fall. Olives are less likely to produce edible fruit in cooler climates, so prune for shape only (*see also pp.144–145*).

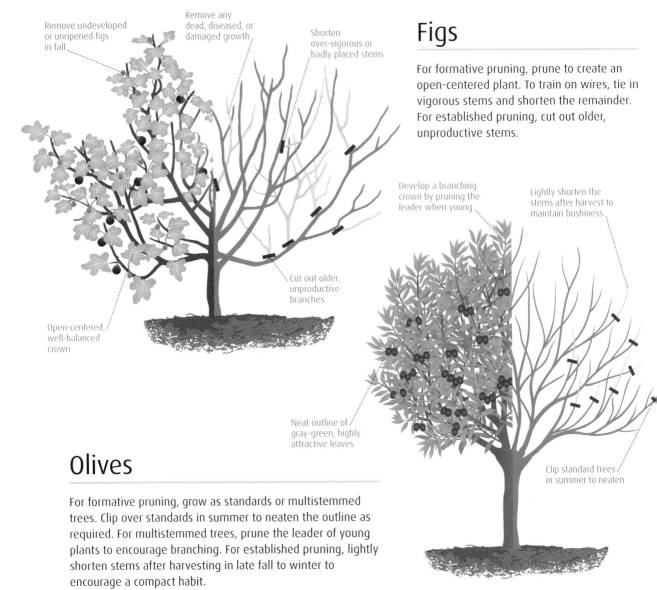

Remove undeveloped or unripened figs in fall

Remove any dead, diseased, or damaged growth

Shorten over-vigorous or badly placed stems

Cut out older, unproductive branches

Open-centered, well-balanced crown

Develop a branching crown by pruning the leader when young

Lightly shorten the stems after harvest to maintain bushiness

Neat outline of gray-green, highly attractive leaves

Clip standard trees in summer to neaten

Figs

For formative pruning, prune to create an open-centered plant. To train on wires, tie in vigorous stems and shorten the remainder. For established pruning, cut out older, unproductive stems.

Olives

For formative pruning, grow as standards or multistemmed trees. Clip over standards in summer to neaten the outline as required. For multistemmed trees, prune the leader of young plants to encourage branching. For established pruning, lightly shorten stems after harvesting in late fall to winter to encourage a compact habit.

Pruning citrus fruit

The citrus group includes lemons, limes, sweet and bitter oranges, and grapefruit. The fruit may take up to nine months to ripen and can be produced at any time, often simultaneously with the next crop of flowers. Fruits are only produced in abundance in warm climates. Trees need little pruning, although stems of young plants can be shortened in late winter to early spring to encourage bushiness (*see also pp.164–167*).

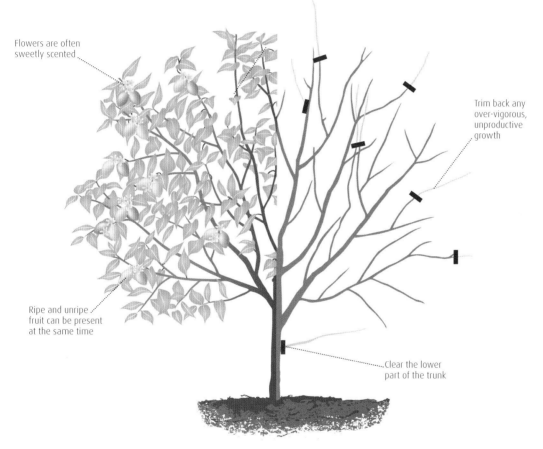

Flowers are often sweetly scented

Trim back any over-vigorous, unproductive growth

Ripe and unripe fruit can be present at the same time

Clear the lower part of the trunk

Citrus fruit

For formative pruning, prune to create a clear trunk 12in (30cm) tall, and a bushy habit. For established pruning, prune to restrict size, if necessary, and remove any damaged, diseased, and crossing stems as you notice them. Dwarf forms of clementine, tangerine, satsuma, and mandarin need little pruning.

TOP TIP: HEAVY FRUIT

For citrus trees that produce heavy fruit, such as oranges and grapefruit, it is best to remove the lower branches from the plants to prevent fruit touching the ground, as this leads to rotting.

Protecting plants and pots

Protecting fruit and vegetable plants from the damaging effects of frost allows tender crops to be grown in cooler climates, and many hardier types to be sown earlier and harvested later, greatly extending the cropping season. If you are using terra-cotta pots, these need protection, too.

Temporary frost protection

Plants in containers are easy to protect at short notice for cold nights in spring or fall. Small pots can be moved indoors, while covering crops in larger containers is an effective way to prevent damage. Half-hardy crops, such as tomatoes, peppers, zucchini, and string beans, are particularly vulnerable to frost damage and need protection, even when acclimatized to outdoor conditions. It is also worth covering many early spring sowings and leafy fall crops to improve their performance.

Designed to keep out the cold, traditional cloches are made of glass, but plastic alternatives are easier to use and safer for crops in containers. Bell-shaped designs are suitable for covering a pot full of young plants, while longer tunnels are useful for raised beds and growing tables. Sheets of floating row cover will protect plants of any size; either support it on wires or canes, or just drape it over plants.

Wrap tender plants with floating row cover if frost threatens. Cover the plant loosely and tie to the pot with twine to stop it blowing away.

All citrus trees must be overwintered in a cool room indoors with plenty of daylight to encourage the fruit to form and ripen.

Overwintering tender plants

Most fruit and vegetables that are not hardy are grown each year from seed as annual summer crops. However, it is worth overwintering citrus trees and chile plants indoors, not only because they won't tolerate the cold, but also because they produce welcome crops in fall and winter. Bring plants in before the first frost.

Place them in a relatively bright but cool room, such as a sunroom or porch, away from radiators and drafts; remember too that windowsills will be too cold at night in winter for many tender crops. Increase the humidity by placing pots on dishes or trays filled with gravel and water. Water plants sparingly.

Protect your pots

As well as protecting plants that are vulnerable to cold nights and frost, some of your pots may also need looking after. Smaller, thin-walled pots made of porous materials—terra-cotta in particular—are most at risk because any material that is porous will absorb water. As the water freezes it expands, causing the pot to crack. Plastic and heavy concrete pots that are not porous are reliably winter-proof. There are steps you can take if you want to protect a potentially vulnerable pot that you would like to keep outdoors year-round. Raising the pot off the ground either on a small wooden trolley, terra-cotta plant feet, or even small stones, will protect it from ground frost and encourage water to drain away from the pot. Then, before adding medium and planting it up, line the pot with plastic bubble wrap (*see p.33*). In colder areas, protect your pots, and any plant roots inside, from hard frost by wrapping them on the outside with a length of burlap as well as lining the inside before planting.

This kind of damage is often seen on terra-cotta pots left outside in winter. Store them somewhere dry, such as in a shed or greenhouse.

Raise pots off the ground with terra-cotta feet, which are available in traditional and more unusual decorative designs.

TOP TIP: STORING EMPTY POTS

Pots that aren't being used over winter are best cleaned up at the end of the fall and stored in a greenhouse or shed. Always wash them first (*see p.33*) and store when dry, ready for the spring.

For overwintering terra-cotta pots, wrap them in burlap sacking secured with garden twine to ensure it won't slip down the container.

GROWING VEGETABLES IN POTS

Many delicious edibles thrive in containers on a patio, balcony, or terrace, bringing community gardening closer to home. Use the advice in this chapter to select a range of crops that suit cramped conditions and discover which plants will best suit your garden site. Also, try new varieties of vegetables that are not available in supermarkets, to widen your culinary experience.

Plant zucchini and cabbages in large containers to produce bumper summer crops and use smaller containers for herbs. Zucchini and chile peppers thrive in the sun, so ensure they get plenty of it.

Caring for your vegetables

Growing vegetables, regardless of whether they are in a dedicated vegetable patch or containers, can keep you busy for many months of the year, starting with pot preparation and sowing seeds in spring, followed by crop care and harvesting through summer and into fall. Use the winter months for clearing up and planning your future crops for the year ahead.

Spring tasks

SOWING SEEDS
Sow vegetable seed in a greenhouse to give both hardy and tender varieties a head start. Begin with eggplants, beets, carrots, cucumber, peppers, and tomatoes.
In mid-spring, sow seeds such as green and string beans, beets, purple sprouting broccoli, carrots, spinach, and Swiss chard directly in containers and cover with cloches if frost threatens.
In late spring, sow tender plant seeds, such as zucchini, peppers, and tomatoes, under cover in a greenhouse.

PLANTING OUT
In early spring, plant out garlic and onion and shallot sets.
Pick out and pot on seedlings of leeks and eggplants, and harden off those that will be planted outside.
Use cloches or cold frames to protect vulnerable seedlings from frost or pests.
In late spring, harden off seedlings and then plant out.
Begin to transplant well-developed seedlings of zucchini, and provide them with protection, using cloches, as necessary.
Plant store-bought pre-grown herbs.

HARVESTING
Harvest overwintered kale, purple sprouting broccoli, and swiss chard, and in late spring begin to harvest new season peas, salads, herbs, and scallions.

ROUTINE CARE
In early spring, give your greenhouse a thorough cleaning. Remove any bubble wrap if the frosts are over, and clean the windows—inside and out. Replace any cracked panes and check that automatic vents are working. Paint any timber panels and wash down the floor and shelves with water and some disinfectant.

Put supports in place for climbing plants; construct tepees from bamboo canes to support beans.
In late spring, prepare seed trays and containers for early summer sowings.
Remove and dispose of weeds as they appear.
Put row cover on young plants on chilly nights.
Water plants regularly.
Top-dress plants in containers if necessary.
Prune perennial herbs such as rosemary, thyme, and sage. Divide clump-forming herbs and replant if necessary.

In spring, sow vegetable seeds in pots and seed trays, depending on their requirements.

Germinate the seeds in a propagator to give hardy and tender varieties a head start.

Summer tasks

SOWING SEEDS
In early summer, sow seeds such as beets, carrots, zucchini, beans, herbs, peas, and radishes. Make late-summer sowings for harvesting in fall and winter.

PLANTING OUT
Transplant all indoor-sown seedlings to their final positions outside in early summer.

HARVESTING
Harvest crops such as beets, zucchini, lettuce, peas, garlic, onions, tomatoes, eggplants, peppers, potatoes, carrots, and Swiss chard. Harvest fruits as they appear to encourage crops such as zucchini and peppers to give a greater yield.

ROUTINE CARE
Feed and water plants regularly, particularly as the weather warms up and the plants begin to bear a crop.
Keep plants well weeded.
Tie in climbing plants and nip out their topmost shoots to encourage bushy growth.
Remove sideshoots from indeterminate tomatoes.
Earth up potatoes and leeks.
Feed, weed, and water greenhouse vegetables regularly and ventilate on hot days to prevent temperatures rising too high. Shade the greenhouse by applying whitewash to the glass and on very hot days damp down the floor by splashing water on it. Remove pests and diseases on sight or buy biological controls.
Deadhead herbs after flowering or keep them trimmed so they don't flower, which is best for herbs like mint or sage.

Fall and winter tasks

SOWING SEEDS
In early fall, sow spinach and Swiss chard under cover. Sow hardy lettuce varieties for winter and early spring picking.
Plant out fall garlic and hardy onion sets and sow carrots and peas to overwinter.
From midwinter onward, sow hardy crops, such as leeks, lettuce, onions, and peas, under cover ready for planting out in early spring.

HARVESTING
Harvest the last crops of many vegetables, including beets, carrots, chiles, green and string beans, peppers, and tomatoes. Kale and leeks should also be ready for harvesting as required, but can be left to stand in the ground for longer.
Over winter, continue to harvest cabbages, kale, and leeks.

ROUTINE CARE
In fall, remove any spent plants and clean the greenhouse after the busy summer months, before bringing in the container plants that will overwinter there.
Clean any empty containers, removing all dead plants—if the debris is disease-free, transfer it to the compost heap. Pile the empty pots in a shed or greenhouse.
Gather up any fallen leaves to use to make leaf mold.
Order seeds, seed potatoes, onion sets, and bare-root plants. Chit your seed potatoes.
If the greenhouse is not heated, line the windows with bubble wrap to raise the temperature and keep out frost. Regularly check plants for pests and diseases, and ensure that their compost is slightly moist but not wet.

As summer slips into fall harvest the last of many crops, including beets, green and string beans, and tomatoes. Cabbages, kale, and leeks can be harvested over winter.

Fresh lettuce

Among the easiest vegetables to grow, lettuce is ideal for pots, where it can be more easily protected from marauding slugs and snails. The widest selection is available in seed form, and the cut-and-come-again types are ready to pick just a few weeks after sowing. Try a mix of lettuce for different textures and tastes.

SALADS

Plants used
'Dazzle' and 'Green Frills' lettuce

Height and spread
H up to 8in (20cm)
S up to 12in (30cm)

Exposure
Sun or partial shade

Temperature
Fully hardy

Harvesting period
Summer to winter

Suitable pot size
6in (15cm) or larger

Container material
Metal, terra-cotta, plastic, baskets

Medium type
Multipurpose medium

Lettuce is not only delicious when picked fresh from the garden, but it also makes decorative features in pots. Fill a container, large or small, with some multipurpose medium and sow your seed thinly on the surface. In small containers, try to sow about three or four seeds of butter, Romaine, and iceberg, which form a heart, or just sprinkle cut-and-come-again varieties more densely, because you will not need to thin these. Sow a few pots each week for a continuous supply of leaves throughout the summer, but remember that seeds will not germinate if the temperature is above 77°F (25°C). When heart-forming varieties reach an inch or so in height, thin them to appropriate spacings, which will be given on the packet of seeds, or a little closer.

CARING FOR LETTUCE

Keep your lettuce well watered at all times, especially in hot weather when you will have to water daily, and move pots to a slightly shaded spot in the height of summer. Lack of water or too much heat will cause the plants to "bolt" and produce long flowering stems—the leaves then become bitter. However, do not allow the medium to become waterlogged or the lettuce will rot. Most multipurpose mediums contain enough nutrients to sustain lettuce for a few weeks, but after that, give them a boost with a nitrogen-rich fertilizer formulated for leafy crops. The main pests to look out for are slugs and snails. Inspect plants every few days and pick off culprits.

*Center: **An old tin bathtub** makes a good home for a collection of 'Green Frills' and dark red 'Dazzle' cut-and-come-again lettuce.*

TOP TIP: HARVESTING LEAVES

Allow the butter, Romaine, and iceberg varieties to mature into solid heads of leaves, and then slice the main stem off at the base with a sharp knife. Cut-and-come-again types can be harvested once by cutting all the leaves off an inch above the base.

New leaves should then regrow, giving you a second crop. Alternatively, pick off a few leaves as and when you need them; more will then grow to replace them. Growing some of each type gives you the best of both worlds.

Choosing lettuce varieties

'**Nymans**' *is a two-toned lettuce with burgundy leaves and bright green bases. Slow to bolt and mildew-resistant.*

'**Winter Density**' *is a compact variety with dark green hearts that offer fresh greens in winter from fall sowings.*

'**Bubbles**' *has distinctive crumpled leaves with a very sweet flavor. Its compact form makes it perfect for pots.*

'**Lollo Rosso**' *has crisp frilly leaves that add color and texture to salads and are a feature in pots in the garden.*

'**Pandero**' *is a tasty mini red Romaine lettuce with crisp leaves that develop a good color and are mildew-resistant.*

'**Tintin**' *is slightly larger than a 'Little Gem'; it has a great flavor and bubbly leaves with a crisp heart.*

'**Salad Bowl**' *has wavy-edged leaves that can be left to produce a loose head, or treat it as a cut-and-come-again.*

'**Little Gem**' *is a popular variety that produces upright, dark green, crunchy hearts with an excellent sweet flavor.*

SALADS

Raising lettuce on a windowsill

For fresh salad leaves on hand whenever you need them, sow cut-and-come-again lettuce in a container on a bright kitchen windowsill. Loose-leaf lettuce cultivars and mizuna and arugula respond well to being sown quite thickly, the baby leaves cut, and the stumps allowed to regrow two or three times.

1 Long, slim pots or fabric bags fit snugly on a windowsill and look attractive in woven willow containers. Fill with medium to about ½in (1cm) below the rim and make drills ¼in (½cm) deep and 2in (5cm) apart.

2 Pour seed into the palm of your hand. For cut-and-come-again varieties, sprinkle the seeds evenly into each drill using your thumb and forefinger. For heartier varieties, sow the seeds more thinly.

3 Cover the seeds lightly with medium and water using a can with a fine spray to avoid disturbing the seeds. Keep the medium moist and, if necessary, thin seedlings to space the plants.

4 When the seedlings are 2–4in (5–10cm) in height, cut them as required, about 1in (2.5cm) above soil level. The plants should then sprout new leaves, which can be harvested about two weeks later.

TOP TIP: PLUG PLANTS

A quick way to freshen up your windowbox or make a change is to make use of plug plants. Buy some part-grown lettuce, water thoroughly, and add to the window box to fill a gap or to replace lettuce grown earlier in the season that are now past their peak.

SALADS

A mixture of salad leaves *and herbs creates a very attractive—and edible—window box display. Keep on picking leaves and replacing harvested or tired plants to ensure that it stays at its best.*

Asian leaves

They may be small but these salad leaves are big on flavor, and when combined with flowers, they make a pretty ornamental display. Easy to grow, the tasty crops are ready to harvest within weeks of sowing— micro greens are even quicker—and all require little care, apart from watering and picking the leaves regularly to keep the plants productive.

Mustard and mizuna

Plants used
Mustard 'Red Giant';
mizuna; *Calendula*
(pot marigold)

Exposure
Sun or partial shade

Temperature
Not hardy below
32°F (0°C)

Harvesting period
Spring to fall

Suitable pot size
Min. 8in (20cm)

Suitable container material
Any

Medium type
Multipurpose
medium

A wicker basket makes a decorative container for a vibrant mix of tasty Asian leaves and orange pot marigolds. The mizuna's serrated leaves contrast well with the rounded, purple foliage of mustard 'Red Giant,' and both will add a peppery kick to salads. The pot marigold doesn't just help to brighten up the basket, its edible petals can also be tossed into salads.

To grow the leaves, mix together a pinch of mustard and mizuna seed, then sow across the surface of a container filled with multipurpose medium. Raise your marigolds separately, sowing seed in pots and transferring a few seedlings into the container when they reach 6in (15cm). Alternatively, buy young plants.

CARING FOR CROPS

Water regularly, especially during hot weather, to ensure that the medium is always moist; dry soil will cause the salad leaves to turn bitter and the plants to bolt. To provide a regular supply of fresh leaves, cut them as you need them from the outside edges of the plants.

Leafy mustard and mizuna should be cropped little and often to keep plants productive and prevent bolting.

TOP TIP: SOWING SALAD LEAF SEEDS

Sow seeds of mustard, mizuna, arugula, or salad leaf mixes in pots filled with multipurpose medium (*see pp.78-79*). When the seedlings are large enough to handle, thin out the weaker seedlings. Don't throw the thinnings away—give them a quick rinse and add them to a fresh green salad.

SALADS

Arugula

Plant used
Arugula

Exposure
Sun or partial shade

Temperature
Frost tender

Harvesting period
Late spring to early fall

Suitable pot size
8in (20cm)

Suitable container material
Any

Medium type
Multipurpose medium

The peppery leaves of arugula are ideal for adding heat to salads or blending together with olive oil to make a fiery version of pesto sauce. Seeds will germinate readily at any time between early spring and early fall, and a single container will provide tasty pickings for several weeks if you harvest leaves regularly. This also prevents plants flowering and going to seed. Although a large pot will provide you with armfuls of leaves, this is a great crop for sowing in small containers, such as window boxes. Water plants regularly to ensure the medium doesn't dry out.

PEST PROTECTION
Cover up your leaves with fine mesh to prevent cabbage white butterflies laying their eggs. These will later hatch into ravenous caterpillars that will munch their way through your crops.

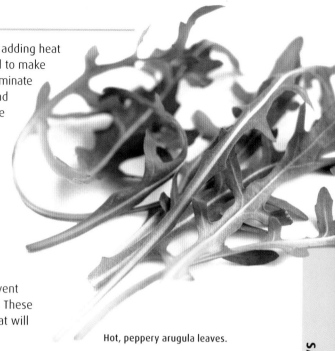

Hot, peppery arugula leaves.

Micro greens

Plants used
Micro greens

Exposure
Full sun

Temperature
Grow indoors

Harvesting period
Spring to late fall

Suitable pot size
A seed tray or recycled shallow container

Suitable container material
Plastic

Medium type
Vermiculite

Micro greens are ready to harvest in just a few days.

Prized by top chefs, micro greens are diminutive vegetable seedlings that are harvested between six and 21 days after germination. They may be small but their flavor is intense. Micro crops grow well in seed trays, plastic seed cells, or other shallow containers with good drainage. Add a 1in (2cm) layer of vermiculite to your container, then scatter seeds liberally over the surface, and do not cover them. Stand the container in a tray filled with water, and leave until the surface of the vermiculite is wet, then drain. Place the container on a sunny windowsill in a warm room, and don't let the vermiculite dry out. Harvest crops with scissors when they have formed their first leaves.

WHAT TO GROW
Lots of vegetables make tasty micro leaves. Try pea pod, sugar pea, sunflower, broccoli, arugula, radish, beet, celery, Swiss chard, and red mustard. Herbs, such as basil, fennel, cilantro, and chervil, are also options.

Spicy salad mix

If you can't face another boring green salad, these three fantastic leaves will perk up your palate and your plate with their distinctive flavors and colorful leaves. Chicory is famously bitter; sorrel has a mild citrus flavor; orach tastes a little like salty spinach. You'd be hard pressed to find the last two in a supermarket, but luckily they are easy to grow.

Chicory

SALADS

Plant used
Chicory 'Treviso Precoce Mesola'

Exposure
Full sun

Temperature needs
Fully hardy

Harvesting period
Summer to winter

Suitable pot size
18in (45cm)

Suitable container material
Terra-cotta, plastic, glazed ceramic

Medium type
Multipurpose medium

Chicory is famed for its bitter leaves, and there are three types on offer. Sugarloaf and red chicory, which is better known as radicchio, are grown for their leaves, while Belgian (or Witloof) forcing chicory produces tender white hearts when deprived of light. All seeds are started the same way. Sow them thinly across the surface of a pot filled with seed medium and cover with ½in (1cm) of sieved medium. Water and place in a sunny site. When seedlings have a few leaves, transplant three into a 18in (45cm) pot. Harvest spring sowings in summer, while seeds sown in summer will be ready from fall through to winter. Cut like lettuce heads.

TOP TIP: BLANCHING CHICORY

Once forcing chicory has developed a good head of leaves in late fall, cut the tops off, leaving a 2in (5cm) stump. Water plants well, then cover the stumps with an upturned bucket to exclude light, and stand in a frost-free place. Your blanched chicons will be ready to harvest after a month.

'Treviso Precoce Mesola' is a really colorful radicchio, with white-ribbed, red-flushed leaves.

Sorrel

Plant used
Red-veined sorrel

Exposure
Sun or partial shade

Temperature needs
Fully hardy

Harvesting period
Spring to early fall

Suitable pot size
12in (30cm)

Suitable container material
Plastic, terra-cotta, glazed ceramic

Medium type
Soil-based medium, eg, John Innes No 2

Difficult to find in stores, sorrel is a perennial herb grown for its tangy, slightly citrussy leaves. It's perfect for adding flavor to green salads or perking up soups. Most sorrels are let down by their looks, but the red-veined variety (*Rumex sanguineus*) has attractive bright green leaves with distinctive red markings. Buckler-leaved or French sorrel (*Rumex scutatus*) is also worth growing for its green, shield-shaped leaves, which have a slight green-apple flavor.

GROWING SORREL
Sow seeds in spring ½in (1.5cm) deep, thinning out seedlings to a final spacing of 12in (30cm). Young plants are also available. Plant into the middle of a container filled with all-purpose medium and keep well watered. Pick leaves when needed, and nip out flowers as soon as they develop, to prevent plants running to seed.

Red-veined sorrel is grown for its mild citrus flavor.

Orach

Plant used
Red orach

Height
H 3ft (1m)

Exposure
Partial shade

Temperature needs
Fully hardy

Harvesting period
Early spring to summer

Suitable pot size
12in (30cm)

Suitable container material
Plastic, terra-cotta, glazed ceramic

Medium type
Soil-based medium, eg, John Innes No 2

Orach is an extremely attractive annual herb that is grown for its spinach-like leaves. It's fast growing and will quickly shoot up to an imposing 3ft (1m).

Sow seeds in small pots of moist medium in late winter or early spring, cover them with a layer of vermiculite and keep moist. Place pots on a warm windowsill to germinate but avoid direct sun. When seedlings are large enough to handle, transplant them into individual pots to grow on. In mid-spring, plant out into large containers filled with medium. Water regularly; if plants become lanky, pinch out the growing tips to encourage bushy growth. To prevent leaf scorch, set containers in partial shade. Harvest individual leaves when large enough.

Red orach (*Atriplex hortensis* var. *rubra*) is a showy plant with reddish-purple triangular leaves. Gold orach has golden foliage, and other varieties produce leaves from magenta to deep purple and fuchsia.

Red orach makes a beautiful plant.

Tangy salad boosters

If your salads are a little on the bland side, spice them up by sowing some fast-growing crops with loads of flavor. Perfect in pots on their own or dotted in gaps around the base of larger plants, radishes, chives, and spring onions are incredibly easy to grow and will shoot up quickly from seeds sown in succession from spring to late summer.

Radishes

Plant used
Radish 'French Breakfast'

Exposure
Sun or partial shade

Temperature needs
Not hardy below 32°F (0°C)

Harvesting period
From spring to fall

Suitable pot size
8in (20cm)

Suitable container material
Terra-cotta, metal, plastic, baskets

Medium type
Multipurpose medium

Perfect for adding a peppery crunch to salads, radishes are easy to grow, and often produce mature crops within four weeks of sowing. There are many different types to choose from, in different colors, shapes, and sizes. Short-rooted radishes can be grown in shallow containers, such as window boxes, while those with longer roots need deeper pots to develop properly.

SOWING SEEDS
Seeds can be sown at any time from late winter to early fall, but early and late sowings need protecting from frost and heavy rain. Either place pots in a greenhouse or cool, light room, or cover them with a bell cloche. Sow seeds thinly across the surface of a pot and cover with a ½in (1.5cm) layer of medium. If seedlings are too crowded, thin out to appropriate spacing. Keep plants well watered, especially during hot, dry spells.

Easy to grow, radishes are a good choice for children to try as they are ready to eat within weeks of sowing.

CHOOSING RADISH VARIETIES

'Scarlet Globe' is a fast-growing variety with round, scarlet roots and crisp white flesh. It is a great choice for a window box or shallow pot, or for dotting around other plants.

'French Breakfast' is a popular radish, with slender roots that have a sweet, mild taste. It requires a fairly deep pot to accommodate the long, pinkish-red roots.

'China Rose', known as the Chinese or winter radish, has long, peppery roots that need a very deep pot. It is favored because it stores well and can be used over winter.

'Cherry Belle' radishes have bright red skins and white flesh, and a sweet, mild flavor. This variety is exceptionally fast-maturing and perfect for small pots on a patio.

Chives

Plant used
Chives

Height and spread
H 12in (30cm)
S indefinite

Exposure
Sun or partial shade

Temperature needs
Fully hardy

Harvesting period
From spring
to fall

Suitable pot size
8in (20cm)

Suitable container material
Terra-cotta, metal, plastic

Medium type
Soil-based medium, eg, John Innes No 3

The pungent, mild onion taste of chives gives a boost to salads and other dishes. You can either buy a young plant or grow your own from seeds sown in spring. Sow seeds about ¼in (0.5cm) deep in a small 3in (7.5cm) pot of seed medium, and place in a heated propagator to germinate. You can then pot the seedlings up outside into larger containers of soil-based medium, such as an all-purpose potting soil, in late spring when the weather has warmed up. To harvest, simply cut the leaves as required just above the medium.

REJUVENATING CLUMPS

Chives spread fairly quickly and will eventually fill their containers. At this stage, either move plants into larger pots, or lift them out and pull them (or divide with a garden fork) into two. Replant healthy sections in new pots of fresh medium.

Chives are ideal for small pots.

Scallions

Plant used
Red scallions

Exposure
Sun or partial shade

Temperature needs
Fully hardy

Harvesting period
Summer to mid-fall

Suitable pot size
18in (45cm)

Suitable container material
Terra-cotta, metal, plastic, deep baskets

Medium type
Multipurpose medium

Red scallions add color to a mixed salad.

Grown for their tangy bulbs and stems, scallions are easy to raise from seed and should be ready for harvesting within 12 weeks of sowing. Seeds can be sown in spring and summer into pots filled with multipurpose medium; either make shallow rows across the surface and sprinkle the seeds into the grooves, or scatter them thinly on top of the medium and cover with a ½in (1cm) layer of medium. Thin seedlings if necessary. The disease downy mildew can present a problem. If you spot a white fungal leaf growth, remove affected plants immediately.

CHOOSING VARIETIES

There are many varieties of scallion available. 'White Lisbon' is popular for its mild white bulbs and stems with green tops, while 'Vigour King' has a hotter onion taste. 'North Holland Blood Red' has striking dark red bulbs and shorter stems with green tops, and adds color as well as flavor to mixed salads and stir fries.

Sweet tomato treats

Home-grown tomatoes are a world apart from those you can buy in a supermarket. Whether you grow young plants from a garden center, or sow your own from seed, you will be picking fresh fruits from midsummer until the beginning of fall. Most tomatoes require large pots or deep baskets to thrive.

MEDITERRANEAN MIXES

Plant used
Tomato 'Tumbling Tom Red'

Exposure
Full sun

Temperature needs
Not hardy below 32°F (0°C)

Harvesting period
Summer to early fall

Suitable pot size
12in (30cm) or larger

Suitable container material
Terra-cotta, baskets, plastic

Medium type
Multipurpose medium

The taste of tomatoes that have ripened naturally over a long season in the sun is unrivaled and makes growing them yourself well worth the effort. Most are happy in pots, as long as the containers can hold sufficient medium and water. Trailing varieties are perfect in deep hanging baskets or large tubs, while cordon types, which are grown as a single stem against a stake, can be planted in big pots or growing bags (*see p.88*).

A good range of young plants are available from garden centers and via mail order in spring, but for a wider choice, sow seeds indoors in late winter. Fill a 3in (7.5cm) pot with seed medium, scatter seeds thinly over the surface, and cover them with a layer of vermiculite. Water the pots and place in a propagator until the seeds have germinated. When seedlings are almost 1in (2.5cm) tall, lift them out of the pot, separate the root balls, and plant each one in a 3in (7.5cm) pot. Keep plants in a light, frost-free place, and when roots show at the bottom of the pots, move them into 5in (12.5cm) pots filled with multipurpose medium. At the end of spring, most tomatoes can be planted outside.

FEEDING ROUTINE

Tomatoes are greedy crops and need to be fed every week with a tomato fertilizer once the flowers appear. This routine should be increased to two doses a week when the fruit has set, and continued until the last tomato has been picked.

Center: 'Tumbling Tom Red' produces bumper crops in large hanging baskets, given a sunny site, and lots of water and fertilizer.

TOP TIP: WATERING NEEDS

It's important that tomatoes are never allowed to dry out or all of your hard work raising the plants will be wasted. Irregular watering can cause the tomatoes to split or hard black patches to form on the bottom of the fruits. This is known as blossom end rot, and is caused by a lack of calcium, which is found in water.

Choosing tomato varieties

'Tumbling Tom Yellow' is perfect for a large hanging basket that will hold plenty of medium and water. The large clusters of sweet, cherry-sized fruit look great cascading over the sides and can be picked all summer long.

'Totem' is a short and compact variety, making it ideal for a large hanging basket or even a deep window box. Its stocky branches carry a heavy crop of bright red fruits. The sideshoots must be removed to ensure a good crop.

'Sungold' produces an abundance of small, sweet, and juicy, bright orange to yellow fruits with very thin skins. Plants are best grown as cordons, with a stake to support the stems, in large pots or growing bags.

'Moneymaker' is a long-time favorite, popular for its ease of growth and dependable crops of medium-sized, red fruits that are borne in large clusters. It should be grown as a cordon in a large container or growing bag.

'Sweet Olive' produces clumps of olive-shaped fruits that hang down from the stems of this cordon variety. It is easy to grow, and will produce a heavy crop in a pot or growing bag, even if you don't remove all of the sideshoots.

'Tigerella' is a decorative variety with orange fruit emblazoned with bright green stripes that looks good in the garden and on the plate. It is a cordon type and produces heavy crops when grown in a large pot in a greenhouse.

MEDITERRANEAN MIXES

Growing tomatoes in growing bags

The medium in vegetable growing bags is specially formulated for optimum growth, but it can dry out quickly. To help overcome this problem, increase the volume by inserting open-ended pots into the holes in the top of the bags and then fill them with good-quality, multipurpose medium.

1 Using a knife, make drainage holes in the base of the bag, and also cut three large circles in the top. Insert bottomless plastic pots (you can make your own or buy ready-made) and fill with extra medium.

2 Transfer your tomato plants to the growing bag when their first flowers are about to open. Plant one tomato per pot, positioning the root ball just below the top of the medium, and water them in well.

3 Add stakes for support, and pinch out all fast-growing side shoots that appear between the leaves and the main stem, as they divert energy from fruit production. Apply liquid tomato fertilizer weekly.

4 As the main stems grow, tie them to the stakes with soft twine. Remove the uppermost tip, two or three leaves beyond the last cluster of fruit on the stem once 4–6 clusters have formed.

5 Keep your tomato plants thoroughly watered throughout the growing season, as the fruits may either split or succumb to disease (see *p.184*) if they receive irregular or insufficient moisture.

6 The fruit will be ready to harvest from late summer to early fall. To harvest the fruit, place your thumb on the stalk joint (knuckle) and bend the tomato upward. Rinse and eat as soon as you can.

The extra medium *in growing bags gives the roots of tomato plants more space to develop and it also holds more water, which will help in the growth of flavorful tomatoes.*

Fruits of the Med

Their plump, juicy fruit and showy blooms make eggplants and zucchini a great choice for a decorative patio display, set among pots of summer flowers and other fruiting crops. Plant them in large containers in a warm, sheltered spot, water them well, and let these Mediterranean delights swell to perfection in the heat of the sun.

MEDITERRANEAN MIXES

Eggplants

Plant used
Eggplant 'Pinstripe'

Height and spread
H 24in (60cm)
S 12in (30cm)

Exposure
Full sun

Temperature needs
Not hardy below
32°F (0°C)

Harvesting period
From summer
to early fall

Suitable pot size
8in (20cm)

Suitable container material
Plastic, terra-cotta

Medium type
Multipurpose
medium

Even before the plump fruits start to form, eggplants make beautiful patio plants, with pretty pink flowers and scallop-edged foliage. Although you can buy young plants, the choice of seed is much greater, and the best option if you want more unusual varieties. To grow plants from seed, fill a small pot with seed medium and scatter a few seeds over the surface. Then cover with a layer of vermiculite and put the pot in a heated propagator. When shoots appear, move the pot from the propagator to a light windowsill. Transfer each seedling into a separate pot when they are about 2in (5cm) tall.

TEMPERATURE REQUIREMENTS
Eggplants will not fruit well during cool, wet summers, as they need a long growing season and plenty of warmth. To help overcome this problem, sow seed in late winter. This gives plants more time to establish, resulting in robust growth and a better crop. You can also extend the growing season by raising them in a warm greenhouse or a conservatory.

'Pinstripe' is a beautiful eggplant variety, with white-striped mauve fruits and a compact habit ideal for pots.

TOP TIP: INCREASING YIELDS

Plants grown outside produce about five fruits. For a good harvest, feed eggplants every couple of weeks with a tomato fertilizer as the fruits start to swell. After five fruits have formed, cut off any side shoots and remove the remaining flowers. Fruits are ready when they are full size and the skin is shiny.

Zucchinis

Plant used
Zucchini 'Golden
Delight'

Height and spread
H & S 24in (60cm)

Exposure
Full sun

Temperature needs
Not hardy below
32°F (0°C)

Harvesting period
From summer
to early fall

Suitable pot size
12–18in (30–45cm)

**Suitable container
material**
Plastic, growing
bags, vegetable
bags

Medium type
Multipurpose
medium

Easy to grow from seed, zucchinis are among the most productive vegetables you can grow on a patio; a single plant will keep you in fruit all summer. Bearing this in mind, don't get too carried away and pot up lots of plants or you will be sick of the sight of the fruits before long.

Start seeds off in early spring by filling a 3in (7.5cm) pot with seed medium. Plant two seeds on their sides, 1in (2.5cm) deep, and cover with more medium. Water, and put the pot in a propagator or on a sunny windowsill. Keep moist and when the roots of your seedlings show through the drainage holes at the bottom, move individual plants into 5in (12.5cm) pots. When there is no risk of frost, place a single plant in a large pot or colorful growing bag. Water regularly and harvest fruits with a sharp knife when they are about 3in (10cm) long.

'Golden Delight'
makes a great patio
feature when grown
in a pretty vegetable
bag. Pick three
zucchinis a week to
keep plants productive.

MEDITERRANEAN MIXES

CHOOSING ZUCCHINI VARIETIES

'Parador' produces large clusters of head-turning golden yellow fruit, which lend a decorative touch to the garden or patio. They have a great taste and mature early.

'De Nice A Fruit Rond' is perfect if you're looking for something a little different. These spherical green fruits are best picked when they are the size of a golf ball.

'Defender' is a tried and trusted favorite, due to its resistance to cucumber mosaic virus. It produces a bumper crop of large, tasty fruits over a long season.

'Venus' is a compact zucchini, ideal for container growing, with uniform, dark green cylindrical fruits that are produced from midsummer through until early fall.

Fiery peppers

If you like spicy food with a bite, turn up the heat in your garden by growing some chile peppers. An essential ingredient of many fiery dishes, chiles come in a range of shapes, colors, and sizes, and will grow happily in containers. Not all peppers are hot, so if you prefer a mild flavor, try the sweet ones.

MEDITERRANEAN MIXES

Plants used
'Cheyenne' chile pepper;*Petunia* 'Million Bells'; Viola; *Lotus berthelotii*; Greek basil

Height and spread
Pepper: H 18in (45cm) S 12in (30cm); *Petunia:* H & S 12in (30cm); *Viola:* H & S 8in (20cm); *Lotus:* H 20in (50cm) S 3ft (1m); Basil: H & S 6in (15cm)

Exposure
Full sun

Temperature needs
Not hardy below 32°F (0°C)

Harvesting period
From late summer to early fall

Suitable pot size
12in (30cm)

Suitable container material
Terra-cotta, metal, baskets

Medium type
Multipurpose medium

*Center: **Match orange chiles** with small violas and contrasting purple petunias. A cascading* Lotus berthelotii *and tangy Greek basil complete this delicious display.*

Peppers are grown for their jewellike, glistening fruits, which come in a range of colors, including red, green, yellow, orange, brown, and purple. Although they can be grown in a pot on their own, peppers don't attract attention until the fruit develops, so create early interest by planting them in a basket or pot with flowers and herbs. Good companions include purple trailing petunias, violas, silver-leaved *Lotus berthelotii,* and basil.

Buy young pepper plants in spring, or grow them from seed sown indoors in late winter. Seeds germinate easily and will need moving into increasingly large pots several times before they are ready to go outside in late spring, when all danger of frost has passed. When plants are about 8in (20cm) tall, or before if they start to lean, stake them with a small cane. Pinch out the tops of the shoots when they are about 12in (30cm) tall to encourage lots of fruiting stems to form. The peppers will be ready to harvest from midsummer and can be removed with a sharp knife or pruners. Picking the fruit regularly helps to ensure the plant puts its energy into producing more crops.

WATERING AND FEEDING

For a good harvest, water plants regularly, especially in hot weather, and feed every two weeks with a liquid tomato fertilizer. Start feeding your peppers when the flowers first appear, often while plants are still indoors before the frosts have passed, and continue until all the fruits have been picked.

TOP TIP: SOWING SEEDS

Fill a 3in (7.5cm) pot with good-quality seed medium and sow a few seeds on top. Cover with a fine layer of vermiculite and place the pot in a heated propagator. After the seeds have germinated, move the pot to a windowsill. When plants are about 1in (2.5cm) tall, move to a 4in (10cm) pot.

Chile and bell pepper options

'California Wonder' *is a very sweet, mild pepper with brick-red fruit, produced on compact plants.*

'Gourmet' *is a sweet pepper with eye-catching, bright orange fruits that appear on small plants, ideal for pots.*

'Pepper Gypsy' *produces tasty, wide, tapering sweet peppers that start green, and then turn orange and red.*

'Alma Paprika' *is a chile pepper with fruits that start yellow and turn red. They have a sweet, mildly hot flavor.*

'Cherry Bomb' *is a chile with round red fruits. They are quite hot, and the plant makes an ornamental patio display.*

'Prairie Fire' *produces hundreds of tiny fruits that make up for their size with an explosive fiery taste.*

'Numex Twilight' *is a compact chile that produces a large crop of small purple, yellow, orange, and red fruits.*

'Aji Amarillo' *makes a compact plant, laden with long, hot chiles that turn from green to yellow, then orange.*

Potted onions and garlic

Onions, shallots, and garlic are staple ingredients in many kitchens.
Growing your own in containers allows you to sample a wide variety
of shapes, sizes, and colors, and to enjoy the freshest flavors.
All members of the onion family take up very little space and
require the minimum of care.

MEDITERRANEAN MIXES

Plants used
Garlic, onions,
shallots

Exposure
Full sun

**Temperature
requirement**
Hardy to 14°F (-10°C)

Harvesting period
Summer

Suitable pot size
Shallots and onions:
24in (60cm)
Garlic: 12in (30cm)
or larger

**Suitable container
material**
Any

Suitable medium
Soil-based medium,
eg, all-purpose
potting soil, with
added grit

GROWING ONIONS AND SHALLOTS

Onions and shallots are best grown from sets (small,
immature bulbs) planted in spring. Choose a large container,
such as a wooden storage crate, that's at least 10in (24cm)
deep and 24in (60cm) wide. Fill with soil-based
medium and make holes 4in (10cm) apart for onions
and 6in (15cm) apart for shallots. Drop a bulb in,
ensuring the pointy end is facing upward, then
cover with medium, firm with your fingers and water
well. The nose of the bulb should be just visible.
Sprinkle over a handful of blood, fish, and bone fertilizer
and keep well watered. In summer, when the leaves
turn brown, crops are ready to harvest. Leave them
to dry on a wire rack for three weeks before storing.

GROWING GARLIC

Best planted in fall or early winter, garlic is divided into two
groups: soft-neck garlic, which forms a mass of strappy
leaves and stores well; and the hard-neck, stiff-stalked types, which are best
used fresh. Split open the bulb and separate the cloves—plant only the largest,
healthy ones. Fill a 12in (30cm) container with soil-based medium, then make
shallow holes, 4in (10cm) apart, around the outside. Place a clove in each,
making sure the flat base is facing downward. Cover with medium, sprinkle
over a handful of blood, fish, and bone, water well, and place in a sunny spot.
Garlic is ready to harvest in summer when the leaves start to turn yellow.

Braid the stems
of your garlic bulbs
and store them in
a cool, dark place.

TOP TIP: DRYING AND BRAIDING GARLIC BULBS

Dried, soft-neck garlic will keep for a long time
if stored correctly. The easiest way is to arrange
a single layer of bulbs on a slatted wooden tray,
keeping them in a cool, dry, dark place, such as
a shed. Those with more patience could take a
tip from the traditional French garlic seller and
try braiding the leaves together to create a
decorative garlic rope. Simply twist off a bulb
when you want to use it.

Choosing onion and garlic varieties

Elephant garlic produces huge bulbs of up to 4in (10cm). Enjoy the mild flavor when bulbs are roasted whole.

Shallot 'Mikor' is perfect for storing. This French shallot has reddish skin and white flesh with a pink tinge.

Shallot 'Ambition' is a long-storing bulb with red skin and white flesh. It is delicious chopped into salads.

Onion 'Red Baron' is a red variety that keeps well after harvesting and has a strong, intense flavor.

Plant onions in a wooden box to lend a rustic note to a patio or balcony. Keep bulbs well watered and you will be enjoying fresh crops all summer.

Ornamental edibles

Leafy Swiss chard, bok choi, and kohlrabi, which also produces delicious swollen stems, form a trio of colorful vegetables that are easy to grow and ready to harvest within a few weeks of sowing. Highly nutritious, use them in the kitchen and to dress up dreary patios or balconies with their vibrant stems and designer good looks.

Swiss chard

TASTY GREENS

Plant used
Mixed chard

Exposure
Sun or partial shade

Temperature
Needs protection over winter

Harvesting period
Spring to fall

Suitable pot size
Min. 12in (30cm)

Suitable container material
Any

Medium type
Multipurpose medium

Many vegetables look rather utilitarian in pots, but Swiss chard's brightly colored stems sit comfortably among more decorative displays. Ruby chard has green leaves with red stems and veins, while 'Lucullus' has green leaves with white stems, but for striking looks, nothing beats the zingy red, white, orange, yellow, pink, and purple stems of 'Bright Lights'.

Young plants are available in spring, but Swiss chard is easy to raise from seed sown from early to late spring. Sow seeds 1in (2.5cm) deep in a small pot of medium. When seedlings have a few leaves, transplant into their own pots; repot again when you see roots growing through the drainage holes. Water regularly and protect plants with row cover or cloches over winter.

HARVESTING STEMS AND LEAVES

Spring sowings of chard are ready to pick after 12 weeks. Harvest what you need by cutting leaves from the outside of the plant. Picking the leaves frequently prompts the plants to produce more, and extends the harvest period.

Feed Swiss chard in containers once a month with a nitrogen-rich fertilizer to keep foliage and stems healthy.

TOP TIP: PLANT A COLORFUL MIX

Rather than growing a single plant in a small pot, create an eye-catching display by planting up a large container with several different-colored chards. Check that the container you choose has adequate drainage. Fill with multipurpose medium and space plants 4in (10cm) apart.

Kohlrabi

Plant used
Kohlrabi

Exposure
Full sun

Temperature
Fully hardy

Harvesting period
Summer to winter,
depending on
sowing time

Suitable pot size
8in (20cm)

Suitable container material
Terra-cotta, plastic
inside decorative pot

Medium type
Multipurpose
medium

You either love or hate the mild turnip taste of kohlrabi, but there's no denying that it makes a fascinating plant for a pot. Pick the young leaves for a salad, or steam as a spinach substitute. Grate the crunchy round stems raw into salads (like celery root), or steam or boil. 'Olivia' is a pretty, pale green-skinned variety, while 'Violetta' has white flesh and a violet-blue skin.

STARTING FROM SEED
Sow seeds indoors in spring by planting three seeds ¾in (2cm) deep in a small pot of medium. After germination, remove the two weakest seedlings. When the remaining seedling has a few leaves, pot it on into a larger container, and move plants to their final pot outside in summer. Water plants frequently, and harvest six weeks after sowing, when no bigger than a tennis ball; much larger and they start getting woody.

'Purple Vienna' is a stunning crop for a container.

Bok choy

Plant used
Bok choy

Exposure
Full sun

Temperature
Fully hardy

Harvesting period
Summer to fall

Suitable pot size
8in (20cm)

Suitable container material
Plastic

Medium type
Multipurpose
medium

An Asian vegetable related to the cabbage, bok choy is steadily increasing in popularity. The leaves can be chopped into salads, or toss both leaves and stems into a stir-fry or lightly steam. Plants can be started from seed, but there's a tendency for them to bolt, so you may find it easier to buy young plants. After a month or so, you can start picking the young leaves from around the outside of the plant. Alternatively, allow the plant to mature fully and harvest the entire head by cutting it off at the base.

WATERING NEEDS
Bok choy has short roots that run close to the surface of the medium, and plants bolt if the medium is allowed to dry out. Apply a mulch of shredded barkor gravel to retain moisture, and water daily in hot weather and in summer.

Leafy bok choy needs plenty of water.

Rich pickings

If you're looking for a nutritious vegetable that's tough, attractive, and can be picked over winter, then look no further than leafy kale. After a heavy frost the flavor will even sweeten up. Spinach, too, can be grown to provide fresh vegetables when there's little else to harvest, but for a real show-stopper, try Chaya, or Mexican tree spinach.

TASTY GREENS

Kale

Plants used
Kale 'Black Tuscany' and 'Dwarf Green Curled'

Exposure
Sun or partial shade

Temperature
Fully hardy

Harvesting period
Winter

Suitable pot size
18in (45cm)

Suitable container material
Plastic

Medium type
Multipurpose medium

Some members of the brassica or cabbage family look rather utilitarian, but kale is queen of the crops. Many cultivars are blessed with great looks and provide color, interest, and food over winter. Perhaps the most attractive one of all is 'Black Tuscany' (often called cavolo nero or black cabbage), with its upright "fronds" of near-black, textured leaves.

In spring, sow seeds indoors into small pots of multipurpose medium, then cover with ¾in (2cm) of medium, and water. When seedlings are big enough to handle, move into individual small pots. In late spring, plant into larger containers outside. If the leaves start to yellow or growth slows, apply a balanced fertilizer.

LOOKING AFTER PLANTS
Keep plants well watered and cover with netting to deter pigeons and cabbage white butterflies. Harvest leaves as required from around the plants, or cut off entire heads. In winter, check plants regularly for heaving, firming the soil around the base of the stems to secure the roots.

Kale 'Black Tuscany' and 'Dwarf Green Curled' provide tasty and colorful leaves over the winter months.

TOP TIP: CHOOSING KALE VARIETIES

'Black Tuscany' has crimped, near-black leaves with a peppery flavor. The green leaves of 'Redbor' turn a deep red, while 'Red Curled' has tightly curled red leaves. 'Red Russian' boasts frilly red and green leaves (left), and the compact dwarf green curled will grow happily in open, exposed sites.

Spinach

Plant used
Chaya, or Mexican tree spinach (*Chenopodium giganteum*)

Exposure
Full sun

Temperature
Fully hardy

Harvesting period
Summer, fall, and winter

Suitable pot size
12in (30cm)

Suitable container material
Plastic

Medium type
Multipurpose medium

There's no point pretending that spinach will stop you in your tracks when you lay eyes on it. It may be highly nutritious, but it's green and pretty dull. Not so Chaya, Mexican tree spinach (not related to true spinach), which is a stunning plant, with triangular leaves and magenta shoots, that will add height and color to a patio display. When young, the leaves are delicious in salads, and mature leaves can be steamed like conventional spinach. The more you pick the foliage, the longer it will continue to crop.

GROWING SPINACH

Sow conventional spinach seeds 1in (2.5cm) deep in pots of multipurpose medium; Chaya is sown on the surface. Thin the seedlings when they are large enough to handle, allowing about 3in (7cm) between plants. Keep pots well watered and shaded, especially during dry spells, as plants will bolt if stressed. If growth slows, feed with a nitrogen-rich fertilizer.

Spinach can be sown throughout the year to provide leaves at different times. For a summer crop, sow from early spring to early summer; for winter pickings, sow seed from late summer to early fall. Plants grown over winter will need protecting from the worst of the weather with cloches or row covers. Harvest by snipping leaves from the outside of the plants.

Lofty Chaya may need staking.

CHOOSING SPINACH FOR CUT-AND-COME-AGAIN LEAVES

Perpetual spinach *is also known as beet spinach. It's a good fall/winter crop with tender, tasty leaves. Plants can last up to two years if picked regularly.*

New Zealand spinach *is unrelated to spinach, but it can be harvested and used in the same way. It makes a bushy plant and can be picked until cut down by the first frost.*

'Galaxy' *has dark green, glossy leaves with a better flavor than the ones that come in those costly supermarket bags. For baby leaves, don't thin out your seedlings.*

'Medania' *has a mild, sweet flavor. It will keep producing succulent leaves as long as you keep it well watered. It also has good mildew resistance.*

Fabulous green beans

Choose from the old-fashioned varieties of green beans with bags of flavor or modern hybrids that promise succulent stringless pods, and you will never want to eat store-bought again. Not only do those grown in the garden taste better, but they can be picked and enjoyed when they are young and tender.

PERFECT PODS

Plants used
Green bean; black-eyed Susan (*Thunbergia alata*)

Height and spread
Green bean: H 5ft (1.5m); *Thunbergia*: H 5ft (1.5m)

Exposure
Full sun

Temperature needs
Not hardy below 32°F (0°C)

Harvesting period
From late spring to early fall

Suitable pot size
18in (45cm)

Suitable container material
Terra-cotta, plastic, stone

Medium type
Multipurpose medium

Many people with small plots understandably give beans a wide berth, but climbing green beans are perfect for tiny gardens, because they can be grown in a large pot up an ornamental obelisk or cane tepee. While some beans are naturally decorative with brightly colored pods, others are less ornamental and can be teamed with flowering climbers to create a striking combination. For example, you can jazz up a plain green bean by planting it with a yellow-flowered black-eyed Susan.

Sow bean seeds indoors in early spring or plant them directly into a large pot of multipurpose medium outdoors, after all danger of frost has passed. Alternatively, buy young plants from the garden center. These climbing beans naturally grip their supports, but it's best to give them a helping hand until they're established by tying them to their supports with soft twine. Dwarf varieties of green bean do not need any supports.

CARING FOR GREEN BEANS
Water plants frugally until they are established, increasing the amount you give them after the first flowers appear and until the last pods have been picked. Also feed plants with a tomato fertilizer biweekly after the flowers form. Beans will be ready to harvest 8–12 weeks after sowing. Picking pods regularly when they're small and tender encourages the plant to produce more.

*Center: **Grow green beans with a black-eyed Susan** in a large pot for a blaze of color and fresh summer vegetables.*

TOP TIP: SOWING GREEN BEAN SEEDS

Place one seed in a 3in (7.5cm) pot of seed medium and put it in a light, bright, frost-free place until it has germinated. Seedlings will be ready to plant outdoors in late spring. Or sow two seeds, 2in (5cm) deep, in the medium at the base of each leg of your support. When the seedlings have germinated, remove the weakest.

Choosing green bean varieties

'Blue Lake' is an old favorite that produces good-sized pods that are tender and stringless.

'Blue Lake 47 Bush' does not need staking. It offers the best of 'Blue Lake' in a compact plant ideal for containers.

'Delinel' produces tasty, slender, stringless beans with a good texture on dwarf plants that don't need staking.

'Purple Tepee' is a dwarf bean that looks and tastes great. Pods are deep purple, turning green when cooked.

'Soleil' is a heavy yielding, delicious dwarf bean that will draw attention with its long golden pods.

'Cobra' is a vigorous variety and requires a large pot. It is valued for its heavy yields of long, tasty pods.

String bean feast

A traditional favorite, string beans are incredibly rewarding to grow. Not only will you enjoy a bumper harvest with the minimum of effort, their flowers are beautiful, too, and there are many tasty seed varieties to choose from, with pods in an assortment of sizes and flavors. Beans will do well in a large pot if given some sturdy support (*see pp.104–105*).

Plant used
String bean 'Red Rum'

Exposure
Full sun

Temperature needs
Not hardy below 32°F (0°C)

Harvesting period
Summer to fall

Suitable pot size
18in (45cm)

Suitable container material
Plastic, stone, terra-cotta

Medium type
Multipurpose medium

String beans are a top-heavy crop, so choose a weighty pot for stability. Depending on the variety, they can grow to 6ft (2m) and will need a support for their long, twining stems, mass of leaves, and crop of pods. A bamboo tepee is simple to make: space four to eight stakes 6–9in (15–22cm) apart in a circle and bind the tops together with twine. Dwarf string beans, which won't grow higher than 24in (60cm), will grow happily in a deep window box or patio pot with only a few short stakes for support.

SOWING, FEEDING, AND WATERING
Start seeds off in small pots indoors in mid-spring for planting outdoors about six weeks later, after the last frost. Alternatively, sow directly into a pot outdoors in late spring or early summer. Sow two seeds 2in (5cm) deep at the base of each stake. Water in well. After germination, leave the most vigorous seedling to climb up the stake and nip out the other. String beans are self-supporting climbers and won't need tying in.

Water plants regularly after the first flower buds appear. If the medium is allowed to dry out, the flowers will fall. During dry weather, mist occasionally with a hand-held sprayer to raise humidity levels. When the beans reach the top of their supports, pinch out the growing tips to encourage more stems with pods to form. String beans are hungry crops: use a seaweed-based feed weekly, switching to a high-potash fertilizer when flowers form.

TOP TIP: HARVESTING

You can expect to be picking beans about three months after sowing. To ensure a constant supply, harvest them every few days while they are young and tender. How long you leave them to grow before picking depends on the variety. In general, if you leave string beans too long on the plant they will become tough and stringy, and if you can feel the beans inside the pods, they will be too old and not worth eating.

Picked when young and tender string beans need little more than lightly steaming and a dab of butter for a delicious dish.

Choosing string bean varieties

'White Lady' produces pretty white flowers followed by thick, tender pods. The flowers are a favorite with bees.

'Painted Lady' bears such pretty red and white flowers that the long, tasty beans are almost an added bonus.

'Polestar' produces masses of tender, stringless beans with smooth pods and bright scarlet flowers.

'Lady Di' has vibrant red flowers with heavy crops of long, slender, tasty beans with no hint of stringiness.

String bean 'Red Rum' *needs a large pot and bamboo cane supports for its mass of scrambling stems. Its beautiful red flowers ensure that it doesn't look out of place on the patio.*

Making a tepee of string beans

Most string beans are climbing plants and take up little bed space, making them a good choice for smaller plots. The easiest way to grow them is up a tepee of canes, and the pot and tepee can easily be incorporated into flowering borders. This also makes efficient use of your vertical growing spaces.

1 From mid- to late spring, plant single string bean seeds about 2in (5cm) deep in small pots filled with multipurpose medium. Water well, and keep indoors or in a heated greenhouse to germinate.

2 Harden off the seedlings (*see p.48*) and only plant out once the risk of frost has passed. Fill a large, deep container with medium and push tall canes into the pot, tying them together securely with twine.

3 Water the beans well. Hold each plant firmly with one hand near the roots and gently knock each from its pot. Using a hand trowel, dig a hole large enough for the plant to sit in at the base of each cane.

4 Gently place the string bean root balls into the holes and fill around the roots with more multipurpose medium. Firm the medium around the roots, making sure the plants are vertical, and water in well.

5 Using soft string, such as natural jute, tie each bean to its cane to help it to start climbing. Pinch out the growing tips when the stems reach the top of the canes to promote new cropping sideshoots.

6 String beans are hungry and thirsty plants. To help conserve moisture and to help nourish your crop, mulch the plants in summer with well-rotted organic matter, such as garden compost.

Plants must be kept well watered *once the flowers appear in order to produce beans; dry spells can cause the flowers or beans to wither and fall.*

Peas and pods

You don't need loads of space to grow peas, snow peas, or sugar snaps. These crops climb vertically up supports in large containers, squeezing onto tiny patios and terraces. Plants will reward you with baskets of tender pods to add to traditional fare and Asian dishes, while young crops are delicious when eaten fresh off the plant.

Peas

Plant used
Peas

Exposure
Full sun

Temperature
Not hardy below 32°F (0°C)

Harvesting period
Summer

Suitable pot size
12in (30cm) or larger

Suitable container material
Plastic, terra-cotta, fabric or growing bags

Medium type
Multipurpose medium

Freshly podded peas eaten within seconds of being picked are a melt-in-the-mouth sensation. As well as tasting delicious, some peas also make decorative patio plants, and really earn their keep in the garden. 'Purple Podded' is a heritage variety with dusky purple pods, while 'Blauwschokker' has red and violet flowers, followed by purple pods.

SOWING FROM SEED

Sow pea seeds 2in (5cm) deep in large pots of multipurpose medium between spring and midsummer. Water well, and when seedlings appear, add supports for the plants to climb up. For an earlier crop, start a few seeds in small pots indoors in early spring, and plant out the seedlings when the frosts have passed.

Water plants frequently, ensuring the medium does not dry out, but see that pots have good drainage by standing them on "feet"; place bags on pebbles. Feed with a tomato fertilizer when flowers appear, and harvest pods regularly to encourage more to form.

White flowers and ripening peas make an ornamental display in a growing bag. Set bags on pebbles to aid drainage.

TOP TIP: STAKING PLANTS

When seedlings are about 2in (5cm) in height, add some supports to prevent plants from collapsing as they grow. Either make a rustic tepee with twigs, use bamboo canes tied together at the top, or, for an ornamental display, use a decorative tripod. Once they get going, peas will grip the supports with their tendrils, but give young plants a helping hand by securing the stems with soft twine.

Snow pea

Plant used
Snow pea

Exposure
Full sun

Temperature
Not hardy below
32°F (0°C)

Harvesting period
Summer

Suitable pot size
12in (30cm) or larger

Suitable container material
Plastic, terra-cotta, fabric or growing bags

Medium type
Multipurpose medium

Snow pea crop throughout the summer.

Grown for their flattened tender pods which are eaten whole, snow peas can be steamed or boiled, or added to stir-fries. There are many tasty varieties: 'Snowbird' has long wide pods that follow attractive flowers, or try 'Oregon Sugar Pod,' which has broad pods with an intensely sweet flavor.

Sow seeds, water, and feed snow peas as you would peas (*see opposite*). Also provide sturdy supports for the stems, which can grow up to 3–5ft (1–1.5m) in height.

PICKING PODS

Snow peas are best picked and eaten young before they become tough and stringy. As a rule of thumb, pick crops when the pods are about 2in (5cm) long. Harvest frequently to encourage a long-lasting supply of pods to form.

Sugar snaps

Plant used
Sugar snaps

Exposure
Full sun

Temperature
Not hardy below
32°F (0°C)

Harvesting period
Summer

Suitable pot size
12in (30cm) or larger

Suitable container material
Plastic, terra-cotta, fabric or growing bags

Medium type
Multipurpose medium

The fat pods of sugar snaps are eaten whole when the peas inside are fully developed. Sweet, crisp, and tasty, they are the perfect ingredient for stir-fries, or you can steam them for a few minutes so that they still retain their crunch. Sow seeds directly into large pots of multipurpose medium outside from late spring to midsummer, and add supports before plants flop.

Sugar snaps require the same growing conditions and watering and feeding regime as peas (*see opposite*). The main pests for all three pod plants are slugs, snails, and birds. Protect containers from slugs and snails with copper bands (*see p.173*) and net plants to keep birds at bay.

WHAT TO GROW

There is a limited selection of sugar snaps to choose from, but it is worth selecting varieties carefully, as some are extremely vigorous and can scale heights of 6ft (1.8m). Among the best for large containers are 'Sugar Ann,' which grows to a compact 30in (75cm), and 'Cascadia,' which reaches 3ft (90cm).

Sugar snaps are easy to grow.

PERFECT PODS

Perfect potatoes

Chipped, roasted, mashed, sautéed, boiled, or baked, potatoes are an essential ingredient in many favorite dishes. Despite being a root vegetable with a sizeable root system, potatoes are relatively easy to grow in pots. Plant in early or mid-spring and they'll be ready to harvest in just a few months.

DELICIOUS ROOTS

Plant used
Potatoes

Exposure
Full sun

Temperature needs
Hardy to 5°F (-15°C)

Harvesting period
From late spring to early fall, depending on type of potato

Suitable pot size
At least 12in (30cm) wide and 12in (30cm) deep

Suitable container material
Plastic; fabric bags

Medium type
Multipurpose medium

Although there are a great array of different potato varieties available to grow in as many different colors, shapes, and sizes, relatively few of them make it on to the supermarket shelves. If you want to sample some of these more unusual, and often delicious, types you will have to grow your own.

PLANTING POTATOES IN CONTAINERS

Before planting, potato tubers need "chitting" to encourage them to produce shoots. In late winter, place the seed potatoes in a shallow tray, an egg carton, or on sheets of newspaper and leave in a cool, light place. The tubers will be ready after about six weeks, when the potatoes can be planted out.

Potatoes need a deep and wide container—a plastic trash can, bucket, or fabric potato bag are ideal. Just make sure it has plenty of drainage holes in the base or the tubers will rot. Put a 6in (15cm) layer of medium in the bottom of your container, then evenly place tubers on the surface, making sure the sprouts are facing upward. Cover with another 6in (15cm) layer of medium and water well. When the shoots are about 8in (20cm) tall, add a second layer of medium, leaving just the growing tips poking above the surface. As the stems continue to grow, keep adding more medium until the container is almost full. Keep your potatoes well watered, especially during hot, dry spells, and feed weekly with a seaweed-based fertilizer (see also *p.110*).

Center: **Large fabric bags** *are perfect containers for growing potatoes in because they are deep and wide, providing plenty of space for the tubers to mature.*

TOP TIP: HARVESTING CROPS

Potatoes are ready to harvest from early summer to early fall. Salad and new potatoes should be lifted while the plants are flowering; main crop types are ready when the foliage dies back. To harvest, tip the container on its side and loosen the soil with your fingers, "combing" through it to scoop up all the tubers.

Choosing potato varieties

'Foremost' *produces neat, round tubers with yellow skins and firm, white flesh. Use as a new and salad potato.*

'Red Duke of York' *has oval-shaped tubers with eye-catching red skins and creamy-white flesh. Good for baking.*

'Yellow Creamer' *is great for boiling. This early potato has oval tubers with pale yellow skins and flesh.*

'Austrian Crescent' *produces small, yellow, kidney-shaped tubers with waxy flesh. A salad potato that stores well.*

'Yukon Gold' *is a large, yellow-skinned potato that is perfect for baking or frying. It has a rich, buttery flavor.*

'Pink Fir Apple' *has knobbly tubers that are impossible to peel, so just scrub them. Delicious served cold in salads.*

'La Ratte' *is an old French variety with nutty-tasting, smooth-textured, waxy tubers that can be eaten hot or cold.*

'Charlotte' *is a great tasting, high-yielding salad potato with slender tubers and firm, creamy yellow flesh.*

Growing potatoes in a trash can

Potatoes taste best when they are freshly harvested. Grow them in deep pots or trash cans like this, and plant "earlies," "second earlies," and "main crops" for tubers over a long period. This will ensure that you have fresh potatoes on your table from late spring to early fall.

1 To sprout ("chit") potatoes, place seed potatoes in egg boxes, with the end with the most eyes facing upward, and set them on a cool windowsill. Plant after about six weeks when the shoots are ¾in (2cm) long.

2 From mid- to late spring, make drainage holes in the base of the can and fill a third with medium. Space five potatoes on the surface, with their shoots pointing up. Cover with 6in (15cm) of medium and water.

3 Add soil around the plants in stages as they grow until the can is full. Known as "earthing-up," this encourages more tubers to form, prevents them turning green and poisonous, and reduces frost damage.

TOP TIP: BURLAP SACKS

A heavy duty burlap sack is a perfect container for potatoes, although it can only be used the once. Plant and grow the potatoes as described in Steps 1–5, but when it comes to eating them, simply cut down the side of the sack in order to harvest your produce.

4 The large, leafy potato plants and developing tubers need a reliable supply of water to produce a good harvest. Feed weekly with fertilizer (*see p.58*) and water well, never allowing the medium to dry out.

5 With consistent watering, potatoes should be ready when the plants flower. Empty the container and harvest the tubers all at once or allow plants to continue growing in the medium, taking what you need.

DELICIOUS ROOTS

The stems of potato plants *are easily snapped. To prevent this from happening when growing potato plants in containers, push a few stakes into the pots for support before the trash can is full.*

Health-promoting roots

You may not have considered growing root vegetables in containers, but as long as you give them a good depth of medium and keep them well watered, they should do well. Beets are a virtually maintenance-free crop, while perennial horseradish requires a little more hands-on attention, but if you're a fan of the fiery sauce it's well worth the effort.

Horseradish

Plant used
Horseradish

Height and spread
H 30in (75cm)
S indefinite

Exposure
Sun or partial shade

Temperature needs
Fully hardy

Harvesting period
Fall

Suitable pot size
Min. 12in (30cm)

Suitable container material
Plastic

Medium type
Multipurpose medium

When planted in the ground, perennial horseradish is an invasive thug, but it can be tamed by growing in a large container. Bare-root plants, also known as "thongs," are sold in spring; young plants are available later in the season. To plant root pieces, fill a pot with multipurpose medium, make deep vertical holes with a dibble, then drop in the roots so that the top sits 2in (5cm) beneath the surface of the medium. You'll fit three root pieces in a 12in (30cm) pot. Cover over with medium and keep well watered. To harvest horseradish, unearth the roots in fall as you require them. The dormant roots can be left in their pots until needed.

REJUVENATING PLANTS
Horseradish is a vigorous plant that will quickly fill a pot. When you harvest it in fall, rejuvenate your plants at the same time. Upturn the pot and remove about half the slender white roots, then replant the remaining portion in fresh medium. These will stir into life in spring, producing a flush of new leaves.

TOP TIP: STORING ROOTS

Horseradish is best used fresh; if you have a glut, bundle roots together and place them in a wooden box or tray covered with damp sand. Put the box in a cool, dark, frost-free place. Alternatively, peel and grate roots in a well-ventilated area, and dry pieces in a low oven for a few hours. Store in an airtight container for 2–3 months.

With its white-splashed foliage, Armoracia rusticana 'Variegata' is showier than the more common green species.

Beet

Plant used
Beet

Height and spread
H 6ft (1.8m)
S 3ft (1m)

Exposure
Full sun

Temperature needs
Fully hardy

Harvesting period
Summer into
early fall

Suitable pot size
12in (30cm)

Suitable container material
Plastic, terra-cotta

Medium type
Multipurpose
medium

If you have never eaten fresh beets before, you're in for a real treat. The roots have a warm, earthy taste that is so much sweeter than anything you will find pickled in vinegar. Tender baby beets are delicious grated raw in salads, while mature roots are best boiled or roasted. Harvest them before they have a chance to develop a woody core—ideally when they are no bigger than 2½in (6cm) in diameter. You can also eat the colorful leaves; harvest them when they are young to add to salads, or steam them like spinach.

If you want to try something different, there is a huge range of variously shaped and colored roots to try, and all have one thing in common—they are easy to grow.

SOWING SEEDS

Sow seed from mid-spring to early summer. Fill a container with medium, leaving a 2in (5cm) gap between the surface and the rim to allow space for watering. Sow seeds thinly across the surface and cover over with a 1in (2cm) layer of medium that has been sieved to remove any lumps. Keep well watered. When seedlings are large enough to handle, thin them out so that plants are about 5in (12cm) apart, to give the roots plenty of space to develop. Use the thinnings in a salad.

Colorful beets are easy to grow from seed; just keep them well watered and you're guaranteed a good crop.

CHOOSING BEET VARIETIES

'Red Ace' grows strongly and is tolerant of dry conditions. It produces dark red roots that are round and uniform in size with a fine, sweet flavor.

'Chioggia Pink' beets are rosy pink on the outside, but when cut open they reveal pretty pink and white concentric circles. Keep well watered to prevent bolting.

'Boltardy' is a very popular variety due to its resistance to bolting. It also matures quickly from an early sowing. Tender spherical roots have a smooth skin.

'Forono' is perfect for slicing due to its long cylindrical roots. Young crops taste particularly good. Delay sowing the seed until mid-spring to prevent bolting.

Crunchy carrots

While we're used to seeing carrots growing in neat rows in the vegetable patch, they do well in large pots too. You just need to match the type of carrot you grow to the depth of medium: long and tapering varieties will need a deep container, while short, stumpy types are fine in shallow pots and growing bags.

Plant used
Carrot 'Mini Finger'

Exposure
Full sun

Temperature needs
Hardy, although young plants may be damaged by frost

Harvesting period
Late summer to fall

Suitable pot size
8in (20cm)

Suitable container material
Plastic, terra-cotta

Medium type
Soil-based medium, eg, multipurpose potting soil

Rounded, stump-rooted carrots are the obvious choice for growing in pots, but if you have a deep enough container you can grow the traditional long-rooted varieties. Ideally, harvest all carrots when young, while they are still sweet and unblemished. Wait for them to color up—in most cases, they will turn orange—and pick them when they are about the width of a finger. Alternatively, grow a miniature patio carrot, such as 'Mini Finger', which has quick-maturing, slender roots.

Early varieties can be sown in early spring, but will need covering with cloches or floating row covers to protect them from the worst of the weather. From mid-spring to midsummer, carrots can be sown outdoors without any protection.

To make growing carrots worth your while, have several pots on the go; sow seeds in each at biweekly intervals. Alternatively, divide up a large container or growing bag and stagger the sowing times in different sections. To sow, scatter seeds thinly across the surface of damp medium—space them about ¾–1¼in (2–3cm) apart—and cover with a ½in (1cm) layer of medium.

WATERING AND FEEDING

The medium should remain damp at all times, but take care to avoid overwatering as this will result in lots of leafy top growth at the expense of root development. Watering after the medium has remained dry for several days will cause the roots to split. Fresh soil-based medium contains sufficient nutrients to ensure a good crop without supplementary feeding.

Center: **Carrot 'Mini Finger'** *produces cylindrical-shaped carrots that will be at their most tender when finger width.*

> ### TOP TIP: PROTECTION FROM CARROT FLY
>
>
>
> When seedlings are thinned out, carrot flies are attracted by the smell and lay their eggs. After hatching, the larvae burrow into the carrot. As a precaution, cover pots with a floating row cover to prevent flies landing and avoid thinning by sowing seed thinly.

DELICIOUS ROOTS

Choosing carrot varieties

'Bangor' *is best grown in a deep container. This main crop variety boasts tasty, smooth, cylindrical roots.*

'Carson' *is a tapering carrot with a sweet taste and a crunchy texture. The crops also store well.*

'Chantenay Red Cored 2' *is a delicious, sweet-tasting carrot. The stump-shaped roots are a deep orange color.*

'Infinity' *has long, slender, roots that are very sweet and crunchy. Can be picked three months after sowing.*

'Amsterdam Forcing 3' *is an old and popular variety with bright orange, sweet-flavored roots. Delicious raw.*

'Autumn King 2' *produces tasty, red-cored roots that have good resistance to splitting. Needs a deep container.*

'Volcano' *is a very tasty carrot that is frost-resistant (good for early sowing) with long, slender, orange roots.*

'Parmex' *is a quick-to-mature, round-rooted carrot with a great taste; roots can be eaten whole.*

Colorful squash

Whether tumbling down the sides of a container or climbing up supports, winter squashes and pumpkins produce colorful fruits to brighten up the garden in early fall. They can be stored for up to six months, providing you with tasty flesh that can be roasted, steamed, or boiled in winter dishes. Small fruits also make ornamental table decorations for the home.

Plant used
'Harlequin' and pattypan squashes; small pumpkin

Exposure
Full sun

Temperature
Not hardy below 32°F (0°C)

Harvesting period
Fall

Suitable pot size
Min. 12in (30cm)

Suitable container material
Plastic, raised beds, growing bags

Medium type
Multipurpose medium

With their wildly colorful fruits in all manner of shapes and sizes, the choice of winter squashes and pumpkins is vast. As well as tasting delicious, the fruits also look great in containers, raised beds, or growing bags on a sunny, sheltered patio.

Either buy young plants in late spring or start your own off from seeds sown indoors. Sow two seeds on their sides, 1in (2.5cm) deep in small pots from early to late spring, and place in a heated propagator. After germination, remove the weaker of the two seedlings. When roots appear at the base of the pots, move seedlings into larger containers, and plant outside after the last frosts. If you don't have room to allow the plants to trail across the ground, train them up supports. Not all are self-supporting, so you will need to tie stems in, and make sure the supports are sturdy enough to take the weight of your plants when they are laden with fruit. Water and feed regularly, especially in hot weather.

RIPENING PUMPKINS
To encourage fruits to develop and ripen, they need lots of light and air, so snip off any leaves that are shading them. Harvesting time depends on the variety you grow, but all need picking before the first autumn frosts.

TOP TIP: STORING WINTER SQUASH

After harvesting your pumpkins and squashes, spread them out on a clean surface in a light, sunny spot, such as a shelf in a cool room or a greenhouse bench, for about a week until the skins harden. This process prevents the flesh from drying out during the long winter storage. Your fruits will keep until spring if stored in a cool, frost-free place on a dry layer of cardboard or clean straw.

Like all squashes, 'Harlequin' and pattypan squashes and small pumpkins require feeding weekly with a high potash formula, such as tomato fertilizer. Your rewards will be these highly decorative fruits.

Choosing squash varieties

'Turk's Turban' is one of the most colorful squashes available. The pale-lemon flesh tastes a little like turnip.

'Jack Be Little' produces up to eight tiny fruits per plant—just the right size for an individual portion.

'Sweet Dumpling' has up to 10 stripey fruits per plant. Either roast them whole or use for soups and stews.

'Winter Confection' has blue-gray skin and orange flesh, which is delicious roasted. Flowers are a magnet for bees.

Small pumpkins may not need extra support, but place heavier fruits in net bags (use those sold with citrus fruit) and tie these to sturdy canes to prevent the stems from snapping.

Winter staples

If you enjoy growing your own food, there's no reason for pickings to come to an end in the fall. Extend the growing season with these hardy crops to add fresh flavors to your dishes throughout the winter months. All can be grown in large pots and are easy to raise from seed or young plants bought from the garden center.

Leeks

COOL-SEASON CROPS

Plant used
Leeks

Exposure
Full sun

Temperature
Fully hardy

Harvesting period
Late fall to winter

Suitable pot size
12in (30cm) or larger

Suitable container material
Stone, growing bags, plastic, wooden crates

Medium type
Soil-based medium, eg, multipurpose potting soil

This staple of the vegetable garden is a handsome plant for a pot, thanks to its upright stems and cascading, glaucous leaves. For a good show and decent harvest, plant enough leeks to supply several meals. Grow them in a few inexpensive plastic pots or large containers, such as wooden packing crates, that are at least 14in (35cm) deep.

Plants prefer a sunny, sheltered site and well-drained, soil-based medium. Sow seeds in pots indoors in mid-spring, and plant seedlings in their final containers in late spring or early summer. Keep crops well watered and harvest from late fall and throughout winter.

TOP TIP: PLANTING OUT SEEDLINGS

Plant leek seedlings in large pots outside in late spring or early summer. First, make holes with a dibble, 8in (20cm) deep and 6in (15cm) apart, and drop a seedling into each. Pour water into the holes and leave to soak away. This draws enough soil over the plants to cover the roots and produce blanched stems.

Depending on the variety, you can pull leeks from the ground between September and April. If they are left too long in spring, they start to flower, then they become inedible as a solid core forms inside the leek.

Winter cabbage and endive

Plant used
Endive

Exposure
Full sun

Temperature
Fully hardy

Harvesting period
Late fall to winter

Suitable pot size
Large rectangular trough or 18in (45cm) pot

Suitable container material
Stone, growing bags, plastic

Medium type
Soil-based medium, eg,multipurpose potting soil

There aren't many vegetables you can pick over winter, but growing cabbages in pots is an ideal way to ensure you have some fresh crops at this time of year. They also make attractive plants that will happily put up with the worst of the weather. There's a good choice of varieties on offer, from smooth-skinned types to the Savoy cabbages, famed for their highly textured, corrugated leaves.

Sow seeds in late spring and plant out the seedlings in midsummer. Use a trough or rectangle container that will fit several cabbage plants and produce a decent-sized crop. Cover pots with netting or row cover to keep out cabbage white butterflies, as their caterpillars will gobble up your crops in no time. Water the plants well and feed with a balanced granular fertilizer when planting out.

GROWING ENDIVE

The frilly leaves of endive are highly decorative, but the bitter flavor is an acquired taste. Sow seeds into large troughs in midsummer, then thin out to space plants 8in (20cm) apart. Pick the outer leaves as required, or allow the whole head to mature and cut it off, leaving a short stump. This may resprout with new growth. Cover with a cloche or row cover in winter to extend the harvest.

Endive looks decorative in pots and has a bitter taste that adds a kick to winter dishes.

COOL-SEASON CROPS

CHOOSING CABBAGE VARIETIES

'January King 3' is a Savoy-style cabbage and a traditional winter favorite, with large, tasty heads concealed between glaucous, frilled outer leaves.

'Jewel' is resistant to bolting and will happily endure tough winter weather to form a loose head of very tasty, smooth, dark green leaves ideal for winter stews.

'Siberia' lives up to its name and will shrug off frost, snow, and any other winter weather conditions without discoloring. It is a Savoy cabbage with a sweet flavor.

'Tarvoy' has been bred to survive the toughest of winter weather. A Savoy cabbage, it produces an attractive, dense, wrinkly head of dark green, nutritious leaves.

Fresh mint

An interesting garnish for boiled potatoes, tangy spearmint is also used to make classic mint sauce, while peppermint makes a wonderfully soothing tea. But why limit yourself to just "minty" mints when you could also be growing spicy ginger, apple, and even chocolate-flavored types? With leaf shapes as excitingly varied as their flavors, plant a selection in individual pots.

HERBS

Plants used
Mentha suaveolens 'Variegata'; *Viola*; *Bacopa* (syn. *Sutera cordata*)

Height and spread
Mentha: H & S 12in (30cm); *Viola*: H 6in (15cm); *Bacopa* S 12in (30cm)

Exposure
Sun or partial shade

Temperature needs
Fully hardy

Harvesting period
Spring to fall

Suitable pot size
12in (30cm)

Suitable container material
Terra-cotta, stone

Medium type
Mix of multipurpose and soil-based mediums

If mint is planted straight into the ground you run the risk of it spreading everywhere. To avoid this problem, keep it safely confined in a container, which you can either stand by the back door within easy reach of the kitchen, or plunge into a gap in the border—just make sure the lip of the container remains above the surface to prevent shoots escaping over the top.

There are dozens of different mints to try. Tashkent mint, *Mentha spicata* 'Tashkent', is an upright plant with heavily textured leaves, while chocolate peppermint, *M.* x *piperita* f. *citrata* 'Chocolate', has dark brown leaves that taste like chocolate. *M.* 'Berries and Cream' has a fruity kick and *M. arvensis* 'Banana', as its name suggests, smells of bananas. If you want to grow several different mints, don't plant them side by side or they will lose their individual scent and flavor.

Looking after mint is easy. Grow in a sunny or partly shaded spot and keep plants well watered, especially during hot, dry weather. Top dress twice a year with a handful of bonemeal.

Picking leaves regularly keeps plants compact and encourages them to produce lots of new shoots. When your plants have finished blooming in summer, cut back any flowered shoots to 2in (5cm) above the surface of the media.

PRESERVING MINT

Mint is best used fresh but you can preserve leaves for use over winter when the plant dies back. Pick shoots, wash well, shake dry, then chop into small pieces and add to an ice-cube tray. Fill with water and freeze. Whenever you need some mint for cooking, simply knock out an ice cube and add it to your recipe.

Lemon mint, Mentha x piperita f. citrata 'Lemon', combines peppermint and citrus flavors and works well in both green and fruit salads.

TOP TIP: NEW PLANTS

When pots of mint become congested you will need to rejuvenate the plant. To do this, upend the container and ease out the root ball. Split it in half, teasing the roots apart, and repot a portion in the same container in fresh medium.

Mint is also easy to propagate from stem cuttings—push 4in (10cm) lengths of stem into small pots of damp medium or stand in water until rooted.

Choosing mints

Apple mint, *Mentha suaveolens, has oval leaves and mauve flowers that appear in summer. Good in mint sauce.*

Horse mint, *Mentha longifolia, is a wild form with gray leaves and spires of purple flowers. Used in aromatherapy.*

Ginger mint, *Mentha x gracilis, has oval leaves with a spicy mint scent that goes well with vegetables and fruit.*

Eau de cologne mint, *Mentha x piperita f.* citrata, *is highly aromatic. Infuse leaves in vinegars.*

Pineapple mint underplanted with violas and bacopa
makes a cottage-style combination for a large rustic container, such as an old chimney pot.

HERBS

Planting an herb basket

Hanging baskets are most usually seen planted with flowering annuals. However, they really can be just as attractive, and productive, when they are used to grow dwarf or trailing vegetables and herbs.

1 To help retain moisture, line your basket with plastic, or a purpose-made liner, before filling the base with medium. Then add some water-retaining crystals and slow-release fertilizer and mix them in.

2 Position upright herbs and vegetables in the center of the basket, with trailing varieties around the edge. In large baskets, you might choose to add some flowering annuals for extra color. Plant closely.

3 Add more medium around each plant, making sure they are firmly bedded in. Top up the basket with medium, but only fill to 1in (2.5cm) below the basket rim, so you can water it thoroughly.

4 Water the plants in well and position the basket in a sheltered, sunny spot. To encourage a good crop, water twice daily during the summer months, and apply a liquid fertilizer every week.

An instant herb garden. *With freshly picked leaves from a choice of mints, some chives, thyme, and a curry plant, there will always be a suitable herb to add flavor to the next meal.*

Calming herbs

Herbs aren't just for flavoring foods, many are also renowned for their calming properties and have foliage or flowers that can be used to make delicately flavored, soothing teas. Fennel, lemon balm, and chamomile are three such herbs. They thrive in sunny sites and make welcome additions to any container garden.

Fennel *Foeniculum vulgare*

HERBS

Plants used
Florence fennel
(*Foeniculum vulgare* var. *azoricum*)
and herb fennel
(*F. vulgare*)

Height
H 6ft (2m)
S 18in (45cm)

Exposure
Full sun

Temperature
Fully hardy

Harvesting period
Leaves from spring to fall; seeds in fall; harvest Florence fennel roots in fall

Suitable pot size
12in (30cm) or larger

Suitable container material
Plastic, metal

Medium type
Soil-based medium, eg, multipurpose potting soil

There are two types of fennel: Florence and the herb. Florence fennel is a biennial grown for its anise-flavored root, which is delicious grated raw into salads or braised, while the feathery leaves of the perennial herb fennel, *Foeniculum vulgare*, add an anise tang to salads. The pungent seeds of the herb, which follow the yellow flowers, are also used for cooking or to make tea (*see below*). As well as the green-leaved species, try the cultivar 'Smokey Bronze' with its bronze leaves and sweet, licorice flavor.

SOWING AND GROWING
In spring, sow Florence fennel seeds indoors into small pots. After the last frost, transfer seedlings outdoors, spacing them 12in (30cm) apart, and cover plants with row covers until the weather warms up. Grow herb fennel from seed or buy young plants. Both types need a free-draining, soil-based medium with a little slow-release, balanced granular fertilizer mixed into the top layer. Keep plants well watered and mulch the surface with garden medium.

Florence (center) and herb fennel make the perfect combination if you love the taste of anise.

TOP TIP: MAKING FENNEL TEA

Fennel seeds have long been used to make a subtly flavored tea that is said to aid digestion and relieve stomach cramps. To make a brew, boil 1 pint (500ml) of water, then add one teaspoon of fresh fennel seeds and leave to steep for 10 minutes. Strain and pour into cups. Serve with fresh orange rind.

Chamomile *Chamaemelum nobile*

Plant used
Chamomile
(*Chamaemelum nobile*)

Height and spread
H & S 12in (30cm)

Exposure
Full sun

Temperature
Fully hardy

Harvesting period
Summer

Suitable pot size
12in (30cm)

Suitable container material
Terra-cotta, stone, plastic

Medium type
Soil-based medium

Chamomile tea is made by adding the fresh or dried flowers of this mat-forming perennial to boiling water. The white, daisy-like flowers appear in summer on long stems above green, feathery foliage, which is highly fragrant when crushed. Roman chamomile (*Chamaemelum nobile*) is the best for flowers— try the form 'Flore Pleno', which reaches 6in (15cm) and produces double flowers. Low-growing types, such as 'Treneague', are used for lawns, but they don't produce the flowers needed for tea.

GROWING GUIDE

Grow chamomile from seed, or buy young plants in spring. Plant in 12in (30cm) pots filled with soil-based medium and stand in full sun. Raise pots up on "feet" to drain and prevent plants rotting, and feed every six weeks in summer with a liquid organic fertilizer. Trim occasionally to prevent stems becoming leggy.

Chamomile is said to soothe frayed nerves.

Lemon balm *Melissa officinalis*

Plant used
Lemon balm
(*Melissa officinalis*
'All Gold')

Height and spread
H 30in (75cm)
S indefinite

Exposure
Full sun

Temperature
Fully hardy

Harvesting period
Late spring to fall

Suitable container size
8in (20cm)

Suitable container material
Terra-cotta, stone, plastic

Medium type
Soil-based medium, eg, multipurpose potting soil

Lemon balm 'All Gold' is ideal for tea.

The essential oil from the leaves of this highly scented perennial herb are widely used in aromatherapy, while lemon balm tea is thought to help relieve tension, aid digestion, and improve memory. The plain green species, *Melissa officinalis*, is rather dull to look at, but the cultivar 'All Gold' is a striking yellow, while variegated 'Aurea' has dazzling green- and yellow-splashed leaves. All three have aromatic leaves that will release their volatile oils at the lightest touch and make soothing teas.

For the best scent, position plants in full sun, and raise containers so they are within easy reach. Trim plants regularly to encourage bushy growth, and remove flower spikes.

WINTER CARE

Lemon balm is a hardy, deciduous, perennial plant but it may suffer during wet winters. Raise containers on pot "feet" and place them in a position sheltered from rain, such as the area adjacent to the wall of a house or a fence.

Evergreen herbs

Herbs that remain green year-round are valuable plants to grow in the garden. They provide color, structure, and beauty all year, and during the winter months they're a mainstay when there's very little else to harvest in the herb garden. Bay is an essential ingredient in the classic bouquet garni, together with parsley and thyme, while sage makes the perfect stuffing for roasted meats.

Bay *Laurus nobilis*

Plant used
Standard bay
(*Laurus nobilis*)

Height and spread
H 6ft (1.8m)
S 20in (50cm)

Exposure
Full sun

Temperature needs
Hardy, but should be protected in hard winters

Harvesting period
All year-round

Suitable pot size
12in (30cm) or larger

Suitable container material
Any

Medium type
Soil-based medium, eg, multipurpose potting soil

A pair of standard bay lollipops in attractive containers is one of the most elegant ways to frame a front door or entrance. A single plant would also make the perfect centerpiece for a group of pots on the patio, or an accent of green in a colorful annual flower border.

Originally from the Mediterranean, bay needs lots of sun and good drainage. Raise containers on pot feet to improve drainage and prevent roots rotting in soggy medium. If possible, move plants to a frost-free place over winter, or, in mild areas, wrap the top in burlap to protect the leaves from wind scorch.

PRUNING BAY

An evergreen shrub with dense-growing leaves, bay is perfect for simple topiary—a cone or pyramid shape is easy to achieve. If left unpruned, plants will soon grow untidy, so clip them with shears in summer. Clear shoots from standard stems by cutting or twisting them off.

Feed bay trees in spring and again in midsummer with a balanced organic fertilizer.

TOP TIP: PRESERVING LEAVES

Bay leaves are best used fresh, but stems or individual leaves can be dried in an airing cupboard. Store the leaves whole in airtight bags or containers for up to a year.

Together with parsley and thyme, bay leaves make up the classic flavor of bouquet garni. Gather a handful of herbs and tie them tightly together with string. Use to flavor soups and casseroles.

HERBS

Sage *Salvia officinalis*

Plants used
Variegated sage (*Salvia officinalis* 'Tricolor'); Strawberries

Height and spread
H 16in (40cm)
S 3ft (1m)

Exposure
Full sun

Temperature needs
Hardy to frost-hardy, depending on variety

Harvesting period
All year-round

Suitable pot size
10in (24cm)

Suitable container material
Any

Medium type
Soil-based medium

Sage is a strong-tasting, aromatic herb that combines perfectly with onions in stuffing for roasted pork and turkey. Common sage (*Salvia officinalis*) has the best taste, but its gray-green leaves make it a fairly nondescript plant for a patio pot. Fortunately, there are many varieties of culinary sage that not only taste good but also have attractive ornamental foliage. Try growing variegated sage, *Salvia officinalis* 'Tricolor', purple sage, *S. officinalis* 'Purpurascens', and *S. officinalis* 'Variegata'.

A native of North Africa and the Mediterranean region, this rough-leaved herb needs a sunny, sheltered spot to set its volatile aromatic oils sizzling. Although it's a shrubby perennial, sage tends to be short-lived, so expect to replace plants every four to five years. Like many perennials, it takes a long time to grow from seed, so either buy young plants from a nursery or take softwood cuttings in spring.

ANNUAL CARE
Common sage is a fairly undemanding plant. Water regularly over summer and keep plants compact by pruning in late spring. Sage doesn't like wet winters, so place pots in a sheltered spot and raise on pot feet. Feed annually in spring with an all-purpose granular fertilizer.

Sage and strawberries *are combined here to create an attractive and aromatic fruit and herb container.*

HERBS

CHOOSING VARIETIES OF SAGE

Pineapple sage S. elegans 'Scarlet Pineapple', *is not a culinary herb, but is worth growing for its pineapple-scented foliage and, in fall, spires of scarlet flowers.*

Variegated sage S. officinalis 'Tricolor', *is a form of common sage that looks and tastes good, with cream, green, and pink variegated leaves. Needs winter protection.*

Purple sage S. officinalis 'Purpurascens', *is a hardy form, with tactile, deeply textured, pungent leaves. In summer, it is topped by tall spires of pretty mauve flowers.*

Common sage S. officinalis, *has aromatic gray-green leaves that are wonderfully useful for cooking. It is fully hardy and survives outside in all but the coldest winters.*

Rich flavors

The aromatic foliage of these flavorsome herbs is at its best on warm, sunny days when the volatile oils they contain fill the air with their pungent scent. Grow thyme and basil in a sunny spot in containers on their own or in combination with other Mediterranean herbs or edible plants for a display that will look as good as it tastes.

HERBS

Thyme *Thymus vulgaris*

Plants used
Golden thyme; tarragon; chives

Height and spread
H & S 10in (25cm)

Exposure
Full sun

Temperature requirement
Hardy, but protect from wet winters

Harvesting period
All year-round

Suitable pot size
6in (15cm) or larger

Suitable container material
Any

Suitable medium
Soil-based medium, eg, multipurpose potting soil

Position pots or hang baskets of thyme close to the kitchen door, or near your outdoor eating area, so that you can pick fresh leaves to sprinkle over salads or grilled meats.

Thyme is a tough little evergreen shrub, and extremely drought tolerant. It thrives in a sunny site in well-drained medium, and you can prevent plants from becoming leggy by keeping the medium on the dry side. Over winter, improve drainage by raising pots on "feet." Feed plants biweekly in summer with a seaweed-based fertilizer, and clip to shape after flowering.

BEST FOR POTS
There are many fabulous ground-cover or spreading thymes, but choose upright types for containers. Among the best for scent, flavor, and good looks are the golden lemon thyme (*Thymus* 'Golden Lemon'), orange-scented thyme (*T.* 'Fragrantissimus'), and *T. pulegioides* 'Archer's Gold'.

TOP TIP: PLANTING PARTNERS

Thyme combines well with other herbs and edible plants. Try growing it alongside red lettuce, chives, and sage for an attractive display in a large container. Apart from culinary uses, thyme makes an excellent companion plant because its pungent smell helps to ward off pests that could damage other crops. Bees also love its pollen- and nectar-rich flowers.

Golden thyme, tarragon, and chives all love the free-draining conditions of a hanging basket.

Basil *Ocimum basilicum*

Plants used
Basil; French marigolds (*Tagetes*); thyme; tomatoes

Height and spread
H & S 18in (45cm)

Exposure
Full sun

Temperature requirement
Not hardy below 32°F (0°C)

Harvesting period
Spring to early fall

Suitable pot size
6in (15cm) or larger

Suitable container material
Plastic, terra-cotta, stone

Suitable medium
Multipurpose medium

Growing your own basil is very satisfying as it is both plentiful and cost effective. You can also experiment with some more unusual varieties. Start these half-hardy annuals off from seed sown in late winter or early spring. Fill a 3in (7.5cm) pot with seed medium, firm down and sow a few seeds over the top. Cover with a thin layer of vermiculite, water carefully, and put it into a propagator. If you don't have one, cover the pot with a small, clear freezer bag and secure with an elastic band. After germination, remove from the propagator or freezer bag. Keep the medium moist, and when the seedlings have four or five leaves, transfer to 3in (7.5cm) pots, placing a few seedlings in each. Move to larger pots when roots show through the drainage holes. Wait until the temperature warms to at least 50°F (10°C) before moving plants outside, although they thrive even better under glass.

KEEPING PLANTS PRODUCTIVE
Basil will continue to produce fresh leaves until the end of summer if you transfer plants into larger containers when you see roots through the holes at the bottom of their current pot. Keep plants bushy and productive by pinching out the stem tips regularly, and remove flowers. Feed plants once a month with a balanced liquid fertilizer, and water in the morning.

Basil mixes well with tomatoes, marigolds, and thyme.

CHOOSING BASIL VARIETIES

'Dark Opal' has purple, oval-shaped, spicy-scented leaves. In the summer it produces striking clusters of small pink flowers at the tip of each stem.

'Horapha Nanum', also known as Thai basil, is a compact plant with narrow, deeply veined, anise-scented leaves that are widely used in Thai cooking.

'Well Sweep Purple Miniature' is a diminutive type of purple basil that forms a low mound. It has great-tasting, green-edged, tapering leaves.

'Minette' is a compact basil that forms an attractive rounded mound, especially in a small container. The dark green leaves have a particularly delicious spicy flavor.

Cooking essentials

Parsley, rosemary, and oregano are three of the most useful and commonly used herbs in the kitchen, but these culinary delights are not just for eating. All possess handsome foliage, and rosemary and oregano produce pretty flowers that attract beneficial wildlife. Site pots near the kitchen door so they are always close at hand.

Parsley *Petroselinum crispum*

HERBS

Plant used
Petroselinum crispum

Height and spread
H 12in (30cm)
S 10in (25cm)

Exposure
Partial shade

Temperature needs
Fully hardy

Harvesting period
All year-round

Suitable pot size
10in (25cm)

Suitable container material
Plastic, stone, terra-cotta

Medium type
Multipurpose medium

If you want an herb to add to winter dishes, sow some parsley seeds in fall and you'll have plenty of tasty leaves to pick over the chilly months ahead. Alternatively, sow in spring for leaves that can be snipped all year. Technically a biennial, parsley is usually grown as an annual, and performs well in pots of multipurpose medium and a partially shaded site. Water plants regularly and pick leaves frequently, which will encourage more to form. Although curly-leaved parsley looks great and has textured foliage, flat-leaved parsley has a stronger flavor and is easier to wash.

TOP TIP: SOWING PARSLEY SEED

Fill a clean container with medium and sow seeds thinly on top. Cover with a ½in (1cm) layer of medium and water. Leave in a cool spot to germinate, which may take up to a month. When large enough to handle, thin the seedlings so they are ½in (2cm) apart.

Curly-leaved parsley makes an ornamental plant for a patio pot, and produces fresh leaves all year-round.

Rosemary *Rosmarinus officinalis*

Plant used
Rosmarinus officinalis
Prostratus Group

Height and spread
H 6in (15cm) S 12in
(30cm) or more

Exposure
Full sun

Temperature needs
Hardy, but protect
in hard winters

Harvesting period
All year-round

Suitable pot size
8in (20cm)

Suitable container material
Any

Medium type
Soil-based medium

Trailing rosemary is a good option for a stone pot.

Ideal for perking up a patio or terrace year-round, rosemary is an evergreen shrub with pungent, needlelike leaves that release their scent every time you brush past. Plants are perfect for busy gardeners, as they require very little care other than watering and feeding annually in spring with a slow-release granular fertilizer. Rosemary produces pretty blue flowers in spring and summer; cut back stems after the blooms start to fade to keep plants compact.

ROSEMARY CHOICES
There are several rosemaries that make good container plants. 'Miss Jessopp's Upright' is tall and thin, growing to 24in (60cm) in a pot, while Prostratus Group has cascading stems. 'Lady in White' has white flowers, 'Majorca Pink' offers pink blooms, and the sprawling, low-growing 'McConnell's Blue' reaches just 16in (40cm).

Oregano *Origanum vulgare*

Plant used
Origanum vulgare

Height and spread
H & S 12in (30cm)

Exposure
Full sun

Temperature needs
Fully hardy, but
protect from
winter rain

Harvesting period
Late spring
to fall

Suitable pot size
6in (15cm)

Suitable container material
Any

Medium type
Soil-based medium,
eg, multipurpose
potting soil

An essential pizza topping, oregano is easy to grow from seed sown in spring, or you can buy young plants from garden centers. Grow in small pots filled with well-drained, soil-based medium, and site in a sunny place. Although green-leaved oregano is the most popular, there are several showier varieties: 'Gold Tip' has leaves with yellow tips, while 'Aureum Crispum' has yellowish-green wrinkled leaves. 'Kent Beauty' is one of the most ornamental—its small pink flowers are surrounded by deep pink bracts.

PLANT CARE
Water plants regularly, but avoid overwatering as the roots may rot in waterlogged conditions. Stand on pot feet to allow excess moisture to drain away, and in winter, prevent roots from rotting by moving plants to a sheltered spot under the overhang of a house wall or into an unheated greenhouse. Trim stems after the flowers fade in summer to keep plants compact, and then give them a boost by applying a liquid fertilizer.

Oregano makes a compact leafy display.

HERBS

Thai herbs and spices

If you enjoy eating Thai food, why not try growing the flavorings for your favorite dishes? Citrussy lemongrass, spicy ginger, and cilantro seeds and leaves are "pantry" ingredients in South-east Asian cooking. All three will grow well in containers on a sunny, sheltered patio, although lemongrass may be more reliable under glass.

Lemongrass *Cymbopogon citratus*

Plant used
Lemongrass

Height and spread
H 36in (90cm)
S 24in (60cm)

Exposure
Full sun

Temperature
Not hardy below
32°F (0°C)

Harvesting period
All year-round

Suitable pot size
8in (20cm)

Suitable container material
Plastic, glazed ceramic

Medium type
Soil-based medium, eg, multipurpose potting soil

Largely grown for the swollen bases of its edible stems, lemongrass is an exotic grass. It makes a fountain of gently arching, strappy foliage, and can even be grown alongside exotic summer flowers and other ornamentals.

New plants are easily propagated from pieces of stem bought from the supermarket (*see below*), or you can raise them from seed sown indoors in late winter. Sow seeds thinly in pots and germinate in a heated propagator. When seedlings are large enough to handle, transplant three into a small pot and stand on a bright, frost-free windowsill. When roots show through the bottom of the pot, move into a larger one, and continue to pot on as plants grow.

CARING FOR LEMONGRASS
In early summer, stand plants outside in a sunny position, and water frequently. Feed biweekly with a balanced fertilizer. In late summer, move your plants to a bright area indoors, and reduce watering, allowing the medium to dry out between each application.

Harvest lemongrass when stems are about 12in (30cm). Cut at the base, leaving a 1in (2cm) stump, which will then reshoot.

TOP TIP: PROPAGATING PLANTS FROM STEMS

Buy fresh lemongrass stems and set them in a jar of water on a sunny windowsill to root. This will take a week or two. Change the water regularly. Once roots have developed, trim the top of the stalks and plant into small pots of moist, soil-based medium. Keep medium damp in summer, but not too wet.

Cilantro and ginger *Coriandrum sativum* and *Zingiber officinale*

Ginger, lemongrass, and cilantro have exotic looks and flavors, yet they are surprisingly easy to grow in containers.

Plants used
Coriander and ginger

Height and spread
Cilantro: H 20in (50cm) S 8in (20cm); ginger: H 36in (90cm) S 16in (40cm)

Exposure
Sun or partial shade

Temperature
Not hardy below 32°F (0°C)

Harvesting period
Cilantro: summer to early fall; ginger: fall

Suitable pot size
8in (20cm)

Suitable container material
Plastic, placed inside a decorative pot

Medium type
Multipurpose medium

Cilantro makes a pretty clump of decorative foliage in either a sunny or partially shaded position in the garden. Grow the cultivar 'Leisure' if you want to use the leaves; for seeds, choose the species *Coriandrum sativum*. All three grow easily from seed sown in early summer. Sow thinly across the surface of a container filled with multipurpose medium, and cover over lightly with a sprinkling of medium. If you want to harvest the leaves, thin seedlings to 1in (2.5cm) apart, and for a crop of seeds, thin to 4in (10cm). Keep the medium just damp.

GROWING GINGER

In spring, start plants off from rhizomes, moving them outside in summer (*see right*). Keep the medium moist at all times, and feed every month with a balanced fertilizer. Plants like high humidity, so occasionally mist with a hand-held spray. Ginger needs high light levels and heat to survive winter, so it is best to allow plants to dry out in the fall, and then harvest the roots.

TOP TIP: SPROUTING GINGER

Ginger is easy to grow from rhizomes. In spring, buy fresh, plump, firm roots from the supermarket with lots of knobbly "eyes." Cut roots into 2in (5cm) lengths, making sure that each piece has at least one eye. Bury single lengths, 2in (5cm) deep, in a small pot filled with multipurpose medium. Water and set in a bright spot. When shoots appear, move out of direct sun and repot as needed. Feed biweekly with a liquid fertilizer. Ginger isn't hardy and must come back indoors at the end of summer.

HERBS

GROWING FRUIT IN POTS

With so many grow-your-own fruit plants to choose from, it's worth taking a little time to explore your options. Some varieties, for example, have been bred especially for containers. All the fruit in this chapter will grow well in a container or growing bag, and produce a good harvest. You can also obtain more advice about specific cultivars from specialty seed companies and nurseries.

Choose and plant wisely. Grow strawberries in large baskets out of the way of greedy pests; buy apples on dwarf rootstock; plant blueberries in acidic medium, and choose a large container for white currants.

Caring for your fruit trees and bushes

Because fruiting trees and bushes can be in containers for many years, routine care is vital if good crops are to be produced. Fruit left to its own devices often produces poor yields, and can be prone to problems.

Spring

PREPARATION

Early spring is your last chance to spray trees with dormant oil to deter overwintering pests.

Top-dress container-grown plants and feed fruit trees and bushes with an appropriate fertilizer.

Water and feed plants regularly as temperatures rise and the plants come into vigorous growth.

PLANTING OUT

Plant strawberry runners when the soil has warmed up and cover with cloches or row cover until after the last frost. To help build up the plants, don't let them fruit in their first year. Pick the flowers off in mid-spring.

Plant bare-root trees and bushes in early and mid-spring, as long as the soil is not frozen. This will be your last opportunity. (Container-grown types can be planted at any time of year.)

Finish planting raspberry canes in mid-spring.

HARVESTING

Harvest any early gooseberries that have been grown under cover.

ROUTINE CARE

Keep trees and plants well weeded, taking care not to damage their roots.

Prune fan-trained peaches and nectarines.

If frost protection is not already in place, cover any tender plants with floating row cover to protect the blossoms. Plum and cherry trees may also need protection.

Hand-pollinate vines or trees that are growing under glass, which may not be accessible to insect pollinators.

In mid-spring, tie in vigorous stems of fig trees and shorten the rest.

In late spring, prune out dead and damaged growth from plum trees and remove any unwanted shoots on trained trees.

Tie blackberries, loganberries, and tayberries into their supports if necessary.

Once flowers appear, cover soft fruits with netting to protect the developing fruits from birds.

Apply a mulch of straw around the base of strawberry plants to suppress weeds, keep the fruit clean, and deter pests such as slugs.

Check regularly for signs of pests and diseases, especially sawfly caterpillars, which may target currant and gooseberry bushes. Deal with them as they appear (*see pp.176–185 for further general information*).

Start feeding fruit trees from late spring, following the instructions on the packet.

Strawberries benefit from a mulch of straw to suppress weeds and a net to keep birds at bay.

Summer

HARVESTING
Harvest tree fruits as they appear, and prune apricots and peaches once the fruits have been picked.
Pick ripe currants and gooseberries as they appear.
Blueberries, strawberries, summer-fruiting raspberries, and currants should be ready for picking by midsummer.

ROUTINE CARE
In early summer, peg down or remove the runners from fruiting strawberry plants.
Thin out fruits of apple, pear, plum, peach, apricot, and nectarine trees.
Net cherry trees to deter birds.
Make sure plants are well watered—especially those in containers—and mulch to conserve moisture and suppress weeds.
Feed plants with high-potash fertilizer as the fruits develop.
Remove dead and diseased shoots and plants, and destroy them rather than composting.
Check for signs of pests and diseases and take immediate action should any appear.
Continue to tie in trained plants, such as blackberries and hybrid berries like tayberries and loganberries.
Prune black currant bushes as well as red and white currants and gooseberry bushes.
In late summer, prune fruited stems of apples and pears. Prune damsons and plums after fruiting.
Once strawberries have fruited, remove old straw and leaves.
Cut out the canes of summer raspberries once the crop has been harvested.

Fall and winter

HARVESTING
Pick fall raspberries until the first frost and harvest any remaining everbearing strawberries.
Harvest the last ripening fruits and store any excess.

ROUTINE CARE
In fall, weed thoroughly around all plants and cut off and remove any damaged or diseased shoots.
Finish any summer pruning of tree fruits and tie in or remove any wayward shoots on trained plants.
Remove any spent plants from the greenhouse and give it a good clean after the busy summer months, before bringing in any tender fruit trees, such as citrus, that will overwinter there.
Cut out old canes of blackberries and hybrid berries after they have fruited.
Cover peaches, apricots, and nectarines to protect them from peach leaf curl and frost, keeping them covered into spring.

Wrap up containers to protect against frost damage.
Prune apples and pears if frost is not forecast.
Prune fall raspberries, gooseberries, and currants.
Cover strawberries with cloches or floating row cover.
Move container-grown plants under cover to encourage an earlier crop.
Take precautions against pests and diseases.
Order new bare-root trees or bushes and prepare the soil for them.
In winter, plant bare-root plants as soon as they arrive as long as the soil isn't frozen.
Remove netting from plants to prevent damage if snow should fall.
If the greenhouse is not heated, line the windows with bubble wrap to raise the temperature and keep out frost. Regularly check plants for pests and diseases, and ensure that their medium is slightly moist but not wet.

Thin the fruit from plum trees in the summer so the ripening plums don't touch one another.

Wrap tender plants and pots in burlap to protect them from frosts over the winter months.

Orchard on a patio

With hundreds of apple varieties to choose from, in an assortment of shapes, sizes, colors, and flavors, it's well worth growing your own. Many favorites are grafted onto dwarf rootstocks, which means they produce full-size fruit on compact plants that are happy growing in large patio containers.

Plant used
Malus 'Fiesta'

Height and spread
H 6ft (1.8m)
S 3ft (1m)

Exposure
Full sun

Temperature needs
Fully hardy

Harvesting period
Late summer
to fall

Suitable pot size
18in (45cm)

Suitable container material
Terra-cotta, stone, heavy-duty plastic

Medium type
Soil-based medium, eg, multipurpose potting soil

You may not have space to plant up an orchard in your garden, but you can still enjoy your own homegrown apples. Compact trees are ideal for large pots on a sunny, sheltered patio, as long as they are not placed in a frost pocket or wind tunnel. Apples generally flower in late spring, and are pollinated by insects that are discouraged by strong winds.

The overall height and spread of an apple is largely governed by its rootstock. If grown on their own roots, apples become too large or produce disappointing crops. To overcome this, they are grafted onto a rootstock, which controls the growth rate and size of the tree. Plants suitable for pots are grafted onto 'M26' rootstocks, which produce trees 8–10ft (2.5–3m) tall, or you can opt for an 'M9' rootstock for a slighter smaller tree. To ensure good pollination, grow a few varieties in separate pots, or buy a family tree, which has several varieties grafted onto one rootstock.

BOOSTING FRUIT PRODUCTION

Water trees regularly during the growing season and give plants a boost in early spring with a slow-release granular fertilizer. Maintain the shape by pruning in winter, removing vigorous shoots and thinning congested stems. Large clusters of fruit result in small apples, as they don't have sufficient space to grow. Although trees naturally drop some fruit in summer, give them a hand by thinning them out. Remove the low-quality large central "king," along with any diseased or misshapen apples.

Center: **'Fiesta' apple trees** *are widely available on dwarf rootstocks, and produce sweet apples in fall. Source apple trees from a specialty nursery where they can advise on things like pollination groups, container culture, and types of rootstock.*

TOP TIP: STORING APPLES

Harvest apples when they come away from the tree with a gentle twist. Wrap in tissue paper and put in a single layer in wooden trays. Or store without wrapping in slatted plastic trays, ensuring that fruits do not touch. Store apples in a frost-free garage or shed, and check fruit regularly for signs of rot.

TREE FRUIT

Apple choices

'Dwarf Honey Crisp' *produces clusters of pretty white blossoms in spring, followed by medium-sized, red-skinned apples that are usually ready to be picked between midsummer and early fall. The fruits are crisp and juicy.*

'Red Falstaff' *produces attractive round fruits that are ready to pick in the middle of fall. Renowned for their superior flavor, these crisp apples store incredibly well, so you may still be eating them in spring.*

'Egremont Russet' *is a highly popular apple with slightly rough, browny-yellow skin and a sweet, nutty flavor when you bite into the creamy flesh. Harvested in early fall, fruits will keep until midwinter if stored well.*

'Pixie Crunch' *produces medium-sized, sweet fruits with greenish-yellow skins that are flushed red. They look very pretty on the tree and are produced in abundance on small plants. They are ready for picking in mid-fall.*

'Improved Ashmead's Kernel' *is a heritage variety that produces highly aromatic fruits with pale yellow skins and a pear flavor. The sweet, juicy apples can be eaten raw or cooked, and they are ready in mid-fall.*

'Ellison's Orange' *is an old variety and many nurseries offer it on a dwarf rootstock. It produces apples with crisp, juicy flesh, and a slight anise taste. The red-flushed, yellow-green fruits are ready for picking in early fall.*

TREE FRUIT

Pears for pots

The wonders of modern, dwarfing rootstocks have made even the most vigorous of fruit trees, the pear, available to container gardeners. As easy to grow as apples, pears just need a little more warmth, sunshine, and frost and wind protection. That said, if you get the site right, your diminutive tree will reward you with bumper crops of sweet fruit.

Plant used
'Terrace Pearl' Pear

Height and spread
H 4ft (1.2m)
S 3ft (1m)

Exposure
Full sun

Temperature needs
Fully hardy

Harvesting period
Late summer to fall

Suitable pot size
Min. 18in (45cm)

Suitable container material
Plastic, terra-cotta, stone

Medium type
Soil-based medium, eg, multipurpose potting soil

Dwarf pear trees may only grow to just above waist height, but they produce masses of foamy white blossoms in spring followed by a heavy crop of delicious pears. Perfect for a big container, the dwarf 'Terrace Pearl' is one of the smallest available. You can restrict the growth of others by training them as cordons, espaliers, or fans. Another option is to grow a duo-minarette, which bears two varieties of pear on short spurs up the trunk rather than on spreading branches.

Plant trees in large containers of soil-based medium, and water them regularly. Feed in spring with a slow-release, balanced, granular fertilizer, and remove any suckers from the base.

THINNING FRUIT

Pears naturally drop some of their developing fruit but will need further thinning. In summer, remove deformed or damaged fruits to give those remaining more space to develop. Fruit will be ready to pick between late summer and early fall. Gently twist off ripe pears from the tree.

The dwarf pear 'Terrace Pearl' *produces a veil of white spring blossoms, and a good crop of juicy fruits on a tiny tree.*

TOP TIP: PRUNING DWARF PEAR TREES

Encourage trees to produce more fruit with careful pruning. In summer, cut side branches to leave 5 or 6 leaves of the summer's new growth. Prune sideshoots growing from these branches to 3 leaves beyond the basal cluster (closely spaced leaves at the base of the shoot), and new sideshoots to one leaf beyond the basal cluster. Also prune in winter to shape the tree.

Choosing patio pears

'Beurre Bosc' is a heavy cropping pear renowned for its slender but juicy, smooth-skinned fruits. Fully hardy.

'Doyenné du Comice' bears large fruits in mid-fall with pale russet, yellow-green skins. Grow in a warm area.

'Humbug' has green, yellow, and pink striped skin. The tear-drop-shaped fruits are very sweet and juicy. Stores well.

'Dwarf Bartlett' has large, pale green fruits with delicious, juicy flesh. Ready to pick in early fall.

Pears need to be planted in large containers with a soil-based medium. Feed them with a slow-release granular fertilizer in the spring and water regularly.

Late-summer delights

Once considered only suitable as orchard trees because of their size, cherries and plums are now available on dwarfing rootstocks. Plant one of these fruiting favorites in a warm, sunny, sheltered spot and enjoy a confection of beautiful spring blossoms, followed by a heavy crop of sweet, juicy fruits from mid- to late summer.

Modern varieties of cherry will grow happily and produce a good crop of fruits within the confines of a container.

Cherries

Plant used
Dwarf cherry

Height and spread
H 8ft (2.5m)
S 3ft (1m)

Exposure
Full sun

Temperature needs
Fully hardy

Harvesting period
Summer

Suitable pot size
Min. 18in (45cm)

Suitable container material
Terra-cotta, plastic, glazed ceramic

Medium type
Soil-based medium, eg, multipurpose potting soil

With breathtaking spring blossoms followed by glossy fruits in summer, cherries make attractive trees for a garden or patio. They are available as free-standing bushes or space-saving, columnar minarettes, which bear fruit on short spurs along a single upright trunk, rather than on spreading branches. You can also train a tree as a fan or cordon against a wall or fence.

Grow cherries in large containers of soil-based medium in a sunny, sheltered site. They flower early in spring and the buds are vulnerable to frost damage, so if a severe frost threatens, bring the tree under cover or wrap it in burlap.

ANNUAL CARE
Keep trees well watered, especially when fruits are swelling and during dry periods. In late winter, give them a good feed by removing the top layer of medium and replacing it with fresh, mixed with a balanced slow-release granular fertilizer. Raise the container on pot "feet" to improve drainage. When fruits are ripening, cover trees with netting to deter hungry birds.

TREE FRUIT

TOP TIP: SELECTING DWARF CHERRIES

Only recently has it been possible to grow cherries successfully in containers. Old-fashioned varieties were too vigorous to have their roots confined, but self-fertile trees grown on modern rootstocks, such as Gisela 5, remain compact. Among the best cherries to try are 'Carmine Jewel' and 'Stella' (*left*).

Plums

Plant used
Plum 'Stanley'

Height and spread
H 7ft (2.2m)
S 3ft (1m)

Exposure
Full sun

Temperature needs
Hardy

Harvesting period
Late summer

Suitable pot size
Min. 18in (45cm)

Suitable container material
Plastic, terra-cotta, glazed ceramic

Medium type
Soil-based medium, eg, multipurpose potting soil

Plums were once the preserve of large kitchen gardens, where mature spreading trees would take up a huge amount of ground space. But plums on a full-sized tree are difficult to pick and protect from bird damage—as with cherries, you need to cover them with netting to ensure you get your fair share of fruits. Modern dwarf trees are much more garden friendly, and plums are now available as small pyramids, minarettes—which bear fruits on short spurs along a single, main trunk—or as fans or cordons trained against a wall or fence.

For the heaviest crops, position your tree in a sunny, sheltered position and water regularly, ensuring the medium in the pot never dries out, especially when the fruits are developing. Feed plants in late winter with a balanced granular fertilizer, and protect them from severe frosts (*for details, see Cherries, opposite*). Plums can be heavy croppers, so check branches regularly for signs of imminent snapping, and have a supply of canes and ties ready for extra support.

CHOOSING ROOTSTOCKS
There are three rootstocks available: semi-dwarfing 'Pixy', which restricts growth to around 7ft (2.2m); the new 'VVA1' rootstock for trees that reach around 8ft (2.5m); and 'Saint Julien A', which produces slightly more vigorous 9ft (2.7m) plants.

Plum 'Stanley' is a self-fertile tree that produces masses of blossoms followed by deep blue plums.

CHOOSING VARIETIES OF PLUM

'Dwarf Burbank Plum' *This fast growing tree produces masses of sweet, juicy, fruit in late summer. A delicious choice for desserts or for making jam.*

'Warwickshire Drooper' *has an attractive weeping habit. Its yellow plums are sweet and juicy and cascade from the branches. Self-fertile, it crops in early fall.*

'Marjorie's Seedling' *has good disease tolerance and is partially self fertile. In late summer, its sweet, purple-blue fruits are ready to pick; enjoy them fresh or cooked.*

'Burbank Plum' *is an American heirloom plum with very sweet oval fruits that are ready for picking in early fall. It has good frost and disease resistance.*

Mediterranean treats

Transport yourself to vacations in the sun by growing a fig or olive tree on your patio. Evocative of Mediterranean landscapes, they can still produce a good crop in cooler climates, given a little care and attention, and even if yours don't bear fruit, both figs and olives are worth growing for their ornamental foliage and graceful forms.

Figs

Plant used
Ficus carica 'Brown Turkey'

Exposure
Full sun

Temperature
Fully hardy

Harvesting period
Summer

Suitable pot size
18in (45cm)

Suitable container material
Terra-cotta, stone

Medium type
Soil-based medium, eg, multipurpose potting soil

Although figs are grown primarily for their fruit, their large, deeply lobed leaves make them stand out from the crowd. They grow quite happily in large pots, and restricting their roots helps to prevent them forming too much top growth at the expense of fruit. More compact plants are also easier to prune.

Buy fig plants in spring and pot up into large containers filled with soil-based medium. Water them regularly and feed with a liquid tomato fertilizer while the fruits develop. Give plants a boost in early spring by mixing some slow-release fertilizer granules into the medium.

FRUITING SEASON

Figs appear in early spring as tiny round growths. These swell over spring and summer, and are generally ready to pick in late summer. A second crop of tiny figs appears around the same time as the first are being picked. In warm countries these will grow fat and juicy, but they need care in a cooler climate if they are to survive over winter for a crop the following year.

Fig 'Brown Turkey' is a popular variety and will grow and fruit well in a large container on a sunny, sheltered patio.

TOP TIP: OVERWINTERING FIGS

Young figs that formed in the summer won't ripen outdoors in cooler climes, so move the pot to a greenhouse or cool conservatory where the fruits can continue to ripen. If you don't have space inside, strip the stems, removing all the young fruits to prevent them from rotting over winter and infecting the plant.

Olives

Plant used
Olea europaea

Height and spread
Olives are available
in many sizes.
A half-standard is:
H 6ft (2m)
S 24in (60cm)

Exposure
Full sun

Temperature
Some are hardy
to 14°F (-10°C)

Harvesting period
Fall

Suitable pot size
12in (30cm) or larger

Suitable container material
Terra-cotta, stone,
wooden Versailles
planter

Medium type
Soil-based medium,
eg, multipurpose
potting soil

Olives are drought-tolerant plants that love to bask in warm, sunny, sheltered sites. Grow one in a large decorative container and enjoy its shimmering silvery foliage, tiny white flowers, which are often scented, and attractive fruits. Water well in the growing season, and set pots on "feet" to ensure good drainage. Feed monthly with a balanced liquid fertilizer to encourage a good crop of olives, and maintain an attractive shape by pruning in midsummer. Remove any dead or diseased branches when you see them.

WINTER CARE
Many olives are hardy, but branches can still be damaged by severe frosts. Bring plants inside, or cover the branches with floating row covers and wrap the pots in bubble wrap. Reduce watering if placed under cover.

TOP TIP: PREPARING OLIVES TO EAT

Olives are too hard and bitter to eat directly from the tree and need preparing to make them edible. There are several methods you can use. Either dry-cure them in salt for several weeks, or soak in salted water for several days. Alternatively, cover them in oil for a few months. Specialty nurseries should be able to advise you on the best method for your olives.

Prune olive trees in summer to allow time for the wounds to heal before their winter dormancy.

Currant trends

Easy to grow, packed with vitamins, and delicious in desserts, pies, sauces, and juices, currants are suitable for new and more experienced gardeners alike. The jewellike, sharp-flavored fruits of white- and red currants will add sparkle to patio pots in summer, while new varieties of black currant produce large, sweet, and juicy fruits on tough bushes.

Red currants

Plant used
Red currant 'Rovada'

Height and spread
H up to 6ft (2m)
S 24in (60cm)

Exposure
Sun or partial shade

Temperature needs
Fully hardy

Fruiting period
Summer

Suitable pot size
Min. 12in (30cm)

Suitable container material
Terra-cotta, stone, plastic

Medium type
Multipurpose and soil-based medium

Although red currants are closely related to black currants, they are, in fact, grown more like gooseberries. These cool-climate plants do well in northern regions and will happily tolerate partial shade, although the fruits will ripen more quickly and taste sweeter if given some direct sun. You can buy container-grown bush and ready-trained cordon plants at any time of the year, but the best time to plant them is in early fall. Choose a sheltered site out of strong winds and avoid frost pockets.

PLANTING IN POTS

Red currants will thrive in pots of multipurpose medium mixed with some soil-based medium. Keep plants well watered when fruiting but avoid waterlogging—place containers on pot "feet" to allow excess water to drain away.

Keep an eye out for raspberry sawfly caterpillars, which will quickly strip the foliage. Check regularly and either pick pests off by hand or spray with a suitable pesticide. Feed and prune as for white currants (*see opposite*).

Red currant 'Rovada' is a heavy cropper; when fruits start to form, move plants to a sunny spot to boost their sweetness.

TOP TIP: CHOOSING RED CURRANTS

There are a number of new varieties of red currant that grow well in containers. Try 'Stanza', a late-flowering variety and good choice for frost-prone areas; 'Rovada' and 'Red Lake' are both disease-resistant and heavy croppers, and also good choices. Check with specialty nurseries for other varieties.

Black currants

Plant used
Black currant 'Ben Lomond'

Height and spread
H 4ft (1.2m)
S 3ft (1m)

Exposure
Sun or partial shade

Temperature needs
Fully hardy

Fruiting period
Summer

Suitable pot size
Min. 18in (45cm)

Suitable container material
Terra-cotta, stone, plastic

Medium type
Multipurpose medium

Tough and resilient, black currant bushes are relatively low maintenance and will fruit with very little effort. New varieties, with 'Ben' in their names, produce large fruits that can be eaten fresh as well as cooked. Plant them in big pots of multipurpose medium and site in a sheltered place, out of strong winds. Plant bushes a little deeper than the original soil mark on the stem; this will encourage new underground stems to form. Feed as for white currants (*see below*).

PRUNING BLACK CURRANTS

For the first few years after planting, just remove any weak and wispy shoots in the spring. After the fourth year, remove up to one-third of the old stems to encourage new growth. If frost is forecast, bring pots inside or cover with row cover.

Black currant 'Ben Lomond' has large fruits.

White currants

Plant used
White currant 'Blanka'

Height and spread
H 5ft (1.5m)
S 24in (60cm)

Exposure
Sun or partial shade

Temperature needs
Fully hardy

Fruiting period
Summer

Suitable pot size
Min. 12in (30cm)

Suitable container material
Terra-cotta, stone, plastic

Medium type
Multipurpose and soil-based medium

White currant 'Blanka' produces sweet berries.

Sweeter than red currants, white currants are cool-climate plants that fruit well in northern countries. 'Blanka' and 'Versailles Blanche' are particularly good varieties. Like red currants, they are shallow-rooted and grow well in large pots. Stand containers on pot "feet" to boost drainage. In dry weather water regularly, ensuring the medium never dries out.

In late winter, scrape off the top layer of medium from the pot and replace with fresh medium mixed with a handful of slow-release fertilizer granules. After feeding, water well and apply a mulch of well-rotted manure to aid water retention and reduce weed growth.

PRUNING WHITE CURRANTS

Prune plants in late winter or early spring. Remove a quarter of the old stems, cutting them down to the base. Reduce remaining stems by a half, cutting to an outward-facing bud. Prune sideshoots back to one bud.

Tart flavors

The stems of rhubarb and plump, juicy fruits of gooseberries make wonderful summer treats when sweetened with sugar and turned into pies, tarts, crumbles, and cobblers. Both plants produce fruit year after year with very little fuss or work, and they not only taste delicious, but make attractive patio plants into the bargain.

Rhubarb

Plant used
Rhubarb 'Timperley Early'

Height and spread
H & S 18in (45cm)

Exposure
Sun or partial shade

Temperature
Fully hardy

Harvesting period
Spring to summer; late winter if forced

Suitable pot size
18in (45cm) or larger

Suitable container material
Stone, terra-cotta, plastic, glazed ceramic

Medium type
Soil-based medium, eg, multipurpose potting soil

Thanks to its massive platelike leaves, rhubarb injects a dramatic note into a patio or garden display. The pink, red, or greenish leaf stalks also taste great when cooked and added to pies and cobblers. Plants are happy in full sun, although they will also tolerate partial shade, and need a big pot and copious amounts of water to thrive. Buy young plants in spring, and repot them into larger containers several times until they reach their final size. If plants start to get too big for their designated position, snip off a leaf or two from around the outside. Rhubarb is generally harvested in spring, although "forcing" produces an earlier crop. Remove old growth when the plant dies back in fall.

FORCING RHUBARB
To produce an early crop of tender pink stems, put a handful of straw over dormant plants in late winter, then exclude light by covering them with a bucket with a solid base. The stems will develop in the dark and be ready to cut after about four weeks.

A young plant needs potting on into increasingly larger containers until it is fully grown. Avoid picking leaves for the first year.

TOP TIP: HARVESTING RHUBARB

Avoid cutting off stems of rhubarb with a knife, because you will be leaving the juiciest part of the fruit behind. Instead, hold the stalk at the base with one hand and gently ease it out of the medium or carefully twist it off with the other; try not to snap it off. You can harvest rhubarb stems between spring and summer.

Gooseberries

Plant used
Gooseberry
'Hinnonmäki Röd'

Height and spread
H & S up to 3ft (1m)

Exposure
Sun or partial shade

Temperature
Fully hardy

Harvesting period
Summer

Suitable pot size
18in (45cm)

Suitable container material
Stone, terra-cotta, plastic, glazed ceramic

Medium type
Soil-based medium, eg, multipurpose potting soil

Forget the sour fruits you may have bought in supermarkets, homegrown gooseberries are truly sweet, with tender skins and melt-in-the-mouth flesh. Producing fruits in midsummer, gooseberries are usually cultivated as bushes in the ground, but you can easily trim them to a lollipop-shaped half-standard in a large container. As well as taking up less space, the area around the stem of a standard can be used for growing other edibles, such as herbs.

YEAR-ROUND CARE
Buy container-grown plants at any time, but you may find they get off to the best start in fall. Pot them up in soil-based medium in sturdy containers that will not topple over as the plant matures. Standards may also need staking.

Water gooseberry plants regularly, especially in hot weather, as dry conditions can result in split fruit. Also work a slow-release granular fertilizer into the top layer of medium in late winter or early spring. When in flower, cover plants with row cover if frost threatens. Half-standards often send suckers up from the base, so either pull them off or cut them back to just beneath the medium. To ensure a bumper crop and to maintain an attractive rounded head, prune stems after picking all the fruit, cutting sideshoots back to around five leaves.

Red gooseberries are both attractive and delicious.

CHOOSING GOOSEBERRY VARIETIES

'Invicta' is a very popular and vigorous variety, producing heavy crops of large, smooth-skinned berries with a good flavor from early to midsummer.

The cultivar 'Hinnonmäki Röd' (see main picture) produces mildew-resistant fruits in early summer. The berries are large, sweet, and aromatic.

'Xenia' is laden with large, red-skinned fruits that are ready to pick in early summer, and add an ornamental touch to gardens. Plants are also mildew-resistant.

'Oregon Champion' has smooth, light green fruits with one of the tartest flavors on offer. This heirloom variety is productive and hardy.

Beautiful berries

Grown for their large juicy fruits, blackberries, tayberries, and loganberries offer a taste of summer. Many are too vigorous for pots, but some new cultivars have been developed in recent years that do well in confined spaces. All plants are grown in a similar way, and it's quite easy to produce a bumper crop of berries.

Blackberry

Plant used
Blackberry 'Loch Maree'

Height and spread
H 6ft (1.8m)
S 3ft (1m)

Exposure
Sun or partial shade

Temperature needs
Fully hardy

Harvesting period
Summer to early fall

Suitable pot size
12in (30cm) or larger

Suitable container material
Terra-cotta, stone, plastic

Medium type
Soil-based medium, eg, multipurpose potting soil

Many blackberries are unruly thugs that need to be tamed by training against a system of horizontal wires. However, there are varieties that make perfectly well-behaved plants for pots, including 'Loch Maree', which produces double pink flowers in spring followed by sweet, juicy berries, and 'Loch Ness' with its single white flowers. Both have thornless stems.

Grow blackberries in a sunny spot, although they will also tolerate partial shade, and plant in a large container. Stake the flexible stems with canes, and water plants well, especially during dry spells. Set pots on "feet" to aid drainage, as blackberries dislike waterlogged soil.

PRUNING PLANTS
After planting, tie in shoots regularly to ensure the plant doesn't grow beyond its bounds. In its first winter, cut back sideshoots made on the main canes to 2in (5cm) to encourage fruiting spurs to form that will carry the berries. After that, each winter cut back to the base the old canes that carried the previous season's fruit.

TOP TIP: FEEDING BLACKBERRIES

Blackberries perform well if given a feed in spring when they start to come into growth. Get plants off to a flying start when planting by mixing a balanced granular fertilizer into the medium, following the application rates on the packet. In following years, apply a slow-release granular fertilizer in spring.

The blackberry 'Loch Maree' is a thornless variety, bred specifically for large containers and small gardens.

Tayberry

Plant used
Tayberry

Height and spread
H: 6ft (1.8m)
S: 3ft (1m)

Exposure
Full sun

Temperature needs
Fully hardy

Harvesting period
Summer

Suitable pot size
18in (45cm)

Suitable container material
Plastic, terra-cotta

Medium type
Soil-based medium, eg, multipurpose potting soil

Although tayberries taste much like blackberries and are grown in a similar way, they actually look more like raspberries. Borne in dense clusters from mid- to late summer, the 2in- (5cm-) long red fruits are sweet and fairly aromatic. In the past it was a struggle to raise tayberries in pots because of their vicious spiny canes, but the advent of thornless varieties, such as 'Buckingham', has made it possible to grow these beautiful berries on a patio or terrace.

GROWING TAYBERRIES

Place a piece of trellis in a container or move your pot against a wired-up wall and train the stems onto the wires. Water plants well during the growing season, but provide good drainage over winter by raising pots up on "feet." Prune canes as for blackberries.

The tayberry 'Buckingham' has thornless stems.

SUMMER BERRIES

Loganberry

Plant used
Loganberry

Height and spread
H: 6ft (1.8m)
S: 3ft (1m)

Exposure
Full sun

Temperature needs
Fully hardy

Harvesting period
Late summer to early fall

Suitable pot size
18in (45cm)

Suitable container material
Plastic, terra-cotta

Medium type
Soil based medium, eg. multipurpose potting soil

Choose a less vigorous variety of loganberry for a pot.

Thornless loganberries bear heavy crops of fruit when grown in large containers, but remember that some forms are vigorous, so choose a slower-growing, thornless variety. A cross between a raspberry and a blackberry, loganberries produce long, dark red fruits, which are usually ready to harvest between late summer and early fall. Apart from their delicious fruits, plants are magnets for wildlife, attracting bees and butterflies into the garden with their nectar-rich, white flowers.

CARING FOR LOGANBERRIES

Place containers in a sunny, open, sheltered site with protection from the wind. To keep plants cropping well, water regularly, especially during the summer, and feed plants with a balanced granular fertilizer in spring.

Train plants against a sturdy support, as for tayberries (*see above*). In fall, after the plants have cropped, cut down to the base all the stems that produced fruit.

Strawberry pot

The quintessential summer fruit, nothing compares with the taste of fresh strawberries ripened to perfection in the sun. Grow these glistening beauties in pots or baskets, and choose a selection of early- and late-fruiting types, or those that produce a continuous supply of delicious berries all summer.

SUMMER BERRIES

Plant used
Everbearing strawberry

Height and spread
H 6in (15cm)
S 12in (30cm)

Exposure
Full sun

Temperature needs
Hardy

Harvesting period
From summer to early fall

Suitable pot size
12in (30cm) container or hanging basket

Suitable container material
Large terra-cotta pot or basket

Medium type
Multipurpose medium with added soil-based medium, eg, John Innes No 2

The true taste of summer, strawberries are a real treat to pick fresh from the garden. The plants grow happily in containers, provided they are watered well and you get to the juicy berries before the birds do. There are many strawberry varieties to choose from, and they are split into two groups based on when they fruit. Most are classed as summer-fruiting varieties, and usually have a single, heavy flush of fruit between early and late summer, depending on the variety. The second group, known as "everbearers," produce berries throughout summer and into the fall.

Strawberries are generally planted in fall or spring. In spring, plant them in pots filled with a mixture of soil-based John Innes No 2 and multipurpose medium, then leave them in a sunny, sheltered spot. In fall, plant up pots in the same way and store in a frost-free place until spring. As well as plenty of water, strawberries need a weekly dose of tomato fertilizer. Protect fruits from birds by covering plants with bird netting.

OVERWINTERING PLANTS

Everbearers run out of steam after harvesting and are should be replaced annually, but summer-fruiting plants will reward you with crops for about four years. After harvesting, cut back ragged foliage, and in fall place pots in a cool, light room, or a frost-free greenhouse to protect plants from poor weather.

TOP TIP: GROWING ALPINES IN WALL POTS

Alpine or wild strawberries are valued for their intensely flavored, tiny berries. Plants produce a light crop of fruit over a long period, but you can ensure a larger yield by growing several plants in a window box or raised trough, where they will be easy to pick. Alpine strawberries also grow well in dappled shade.

*Center: **Plant a large terra-cotta pot** with everbearing berries for a continuous supply of sweet fruits from midsummer into fall.*

Strawberry choices

'Cambridge Favourite' produces sweet berries that can be left on the plant longer than most without rotting.

'Albion' is an everbearing disease-resistant variety with bright red, cone-shaped, sweet, tasty fruits.

'Mara des Bois' is an everbearer, with aromatic, sweetly flavored fruits borne from midsummer to fall.

'Alstar' is a vigorous, leafy plant, and produces masses of large, dark red berries in midsummer.

'Ozark Beauty', an everbearing variety, produces a heavy crop of large, sweet, and juicy fruits from midsummer.

'Elsanta' is a very popular variety with large, orange-red, tasty berries that are borne in great profusion in midsummer.

'The Jewel' bears heavy crops of very sweet red berries with firm flesh in the middle of the summer.

Alpine strawberries may be a fraction of the size of named varieties, but they are aromatic and deliciously sweet.

SUMMER BERRIES

Planting a strawberry basket

Growing strawberries in baskets has several advantages. Not only are fruits raised up to head height, which makes picking them nice and easy, but they are also well out of reach of many pests. In addition, they should not rot, as they have no direct contact with the soil.

1 Place the basket in a pot to keep it stable while planting it up, and if it doesn't have an integral liner, line with heavy-duty plastic to both retain the medium and help keep it moist (*see pp.32–33*).

2 Half-fill the strawberry basket with a mixture of soil-based John Innes No 2 and multipurpose medium. Add some slow-release fertilizer and water-retaining gel crystals to the medium.

3 Plunge the strawberry plants in a bucket of water to ensure that the root balls are sufficiently moist. Then gently remove them from their pots and tease out the roots a little to loosen them.

4 Space the strawberries evenly around the basket. Then plant them to the same depth as they were in their pots and so that the top of the root balls are 1in (2.5cm) below the rim of the basket.

5 Top up the strawberry basket with enough medium to reach 1in (2.5cm) below the rim, to allow space for watering. When the fruit starts to ripen, cover it with netting to protect it from birds.

6 Soak the basket well and allow the water to drain before suspending it from a sturdy and well-secured bracket or hook. Water daily in warm weather and apply a liquid tomato fertilizer every two weeks.

Hang the basket *in a sunny sheltered spot and expect to be able to start rewarding yourself with beautiful moist berries beginning in May.*

Berries blue
Blueberry and honeyberry

Known as "superfoods" due to their high vitamin content, these delicious berries are produced on compact shrubs that grow happily in patio pots. Apart from the beautiful blue fruits, many offer a long season of interest, boasting attractive flowers and foliage, and fiery fall colors.

Plants used
Blueberry and honeyberry

Height and spread
Blueberry: H & S 3ft (1m); Honeyberry: H & S up to 5ft (1.5m)

Exposure
Sun or partial shade

Temperature needs
Fully hardy

Harvesting period
Summer

Suitable pot size
18in (45cm)

Suitable container material
Any nonporous material

Medium type
Blueberry: soil-based acidic medium; Honeyberry: soil-based medium

GROWING BLUEBERRIES

Healthy blueberries are the perfect fruits for a small garden or patio, providing a wealth of interest. In spring, plants bear a profusion of tiny white flowers, followed by the blue summer berries, and, in some varieties, fiery scarlet fall foliage.

Grow blueberries in pots of soil-based acidic medium, and water using water from a rain barrel—only use tap water as a last resort during periods of drought. While in growth, give them a biweekly dose of balanced feed formulated for acid-loving plants, and sit pots in full sun or partial shade.

Select a plant, from the many varieties available, that is naturally compact and suited to a pot. Some are not self-fertile, and so you will need to buy two plants. In a large pot, you could team them with cranberries, which like the same growing conditions and will extend the fruiting season until fall.

GROWING HONEYBERRIES

Native to Siberia, honeyberry plants are extremely hardy. They are grown for their large fruits that look and taste like blueberries, and the best results are achieved by growing two plants together. Honeyberries also do well in pots of soil-based medium and you can use water straight from the tap. Apply a slow-release granular feed in spring, and tomato fertilizer every two weeks after the flowers appear.

TOP TIP: PRESERVING

When they are ripe, remove berries from plants by gently pulling them from the stems. They are best eaten fresh or cooked in desserts. However, berries will keep fresh for several weeks in the refrigerator. Place them in a single layer in a storage container, ensuring that they do not rest on top of one another or the weight could cause bruising and result in rotting. If you end up with a glut, berries can also be frozen.

Blueberries need acid soil but they are easily grown in pots if your garden's conditions are alkaline.

Berry selections

Blueberry 'Brigitta' *has richly flavored fruits that ripen at the end of summer. Grow another variety with it.*

Blueberry 'Earliblue' *makes a vigorous bush that is covered with large, juicy berries in midsummer.*

Blueberry 'Toro' *produces a bumper crop of berries over the summer, and has bright red fall foliage.*

Honeyberry *bears long, oval berries in early summer with a blueberry flavor and honey aftertaste.*

Delicious plump berries *are produced in abundance in summer, but birds also enjoy these juicy fruits. To prevent your crop disappearing, cover plants with bird netting.*

Ripening raspberries

You could be forgiven for thinking that raspberries demand a lot of space—visit any garden and you will see vast rows of canes. However, for the majority of people this actually yields too much fruit each year, whereas growing raspberry canes in a container can easily meet your needs.

SUMMER AND FALL BERRIES

Plant used
Summer raspberry 'Octavia'

Exposure
Sun or partial shade

Temperature needs
Fully hardy

Harvesting period
July to August

Suitable pot size
12in (30cm)

Suitable container material
Plastic, terra-cotta

Compost type
Soil-based compost, eg, multipurpose potting soil

Summer-fruiting raspberries crop from mid- to late summer; fall varieties fruit from late summer to mid-fall, so plant both types to ensure you have the longest harvest. Summer raspberries grown in pots can be trained up a bamboo pole, whereas fall-fruiting varieties can be grown free-standing. They are generally sold as bare-roots or root-wrapped—lifted from the ground and bundled together loosely in medium.

Plant up to three canes in a 12in (30cm) diameter container in late fall, although winter and early spring are also an option. Use a soil-based medium and feed monthly during the growing season with a liquid general-purpose fertilizer.

WATERING AND PRUNING

Keep plants well watered during summer, even daily during dry spells, and avoid splashing the stems, which spreads disease. As soon as the fruit start to ripen, protect them from birds. Cover plants with a cage or using netting, held taut using canes to prevent snaring birds. They are less interested in fall-fruiting varieties, however, which can even be grown without protection.

Prune summer-fruiting raspberries straight after the last fruits have been harvested, cutting the fruited canes to the base. Younger, unfruited stems, produced that summer, should be tied to the wires in their place. Keep only the strongest and tie them in 4in (10cm) apart, to fruit next year. For fall raspberries, cut the canes to ground level in February. Reduce the number of canes slightly in summer if they become overcrowded.

Center: **Both summer- and fall-fruiting varieties** *(here, the summer raspberry 'Octavia') are worth growing in containers, allowing you to enjoy sweet, tart berries from midsummer right through to the first frost.*

TOP TIP: HARVESTING

The berries are ready as soon as they turn fully red or yellow, depending on variety, and pull easily from the plant. Avoid picking on rainy days as wet fruit does not store well. Check plants daily to ensure you harvest them at the perfect point of ripeness.

Choosing raspberry varieties

'Joan J' is a spine-free and self-supporting fall variety. It is compact and suitable for containers. Keep it well watered and fed if pot grown.

'Tulameen' fruits in summer over several weeks, and is a good choice for cooler areas.

'Octavia' bears fruit all along the canes and is one of the last raspberries to finish cropping in the summer.

'Fall Bliss' is shorter than most and can be grown without support. It fruits freely, well into fall.

'Cascade Delight' is a free-fruiting summer raspberry, with large and juicy rich-tasting berries.

'Polka' bears especially large and sweet fruit that are produced in abundance in fall until November.

'Fall Gold' crops in fall, producing deliciously sweet yellow fruits that won't stain your fingers.

SUMMER AND FALL BERRIES

Juicy fruits

Biting into a sweet, juicy peach or apricot that has ripened to perfection is a real treat. These days you don't need a heated greenhouse to enjoy such homegrown delights, as there are many new cultivars that will crop well in cooler climates. Grow them as a free-standing tree or fan-train the branches against a south- or west-facing wall for speedy ripening.

Peaches

Plant used
Dwarf peach

Height and spread
H 5ft (1.5m)
S 3ft (1m)

Exposure
Full sun

Temperature
Fully hardy

Harvesting period
Summer

Suitable pot size
Min. 18in (45cm)

Suitable container material
Any

Medium type
Soil-based medium, eg, multipurpose potting soil

Choose a peach tree on dwarfing rootstock (*see below*) and grow as a free-standing tree, or buy a partially trained fan to grow against a wall or fence. You can plant bare-root trees in late fall or early spring, while container-grown trees can be planted year-round.

For maximum flavor and quick ripening, peaches require a sunny, sheltered site. Your tree will also need regular watering and feeding. In spring, remove the top layer of medium in the pot and replace with fresh. Add a slow-release, granular fertilizer and top-dress with well-rotted manure. When fruiting, give trees a weekly boost with tomato fertilizer. Protect plants from rainfall in late winter and early spring to avoid problems with leaf curl, and bring blossoming trees under cover or wrap in row cover if frost threatens.

BUMPER HARVEST
When your peach tree starts to blossom, spend a few minutes pressing the bristles of a small, soft paintbrush into every flower. This will improve pollination and boost your crops.

TOP TIP: DWARF ROOTSTOCKS
Trees grown on the dwarfing rootstock 'Saint Julien A' are ideal for containers; their size is naturally limited to 4–5ft (1.2–1.5m) without the need for heavy pruning. 'Duke of York' has delicious, pale juicy flesh; 'Champion' is an old favorite with excellent flavor; 'Garden Lady' has sweet, juicy, yellow-fleshed fruit; yellow-fleshed 'Bonanza' is a heavy cropper. Fruit trees often need other trees close by to aid pollination, but these peaches are all self-fertile.

TENDER FRUIT

Pot-grown peaches often carry bumper crops; you will need to thin out the fruits to keep the branches from snapping.

Apricots

Plant used
Apricot

Height and spread
H 5ft (1.5m)
S 3ft (1m)

Exposure
Full sun

Temperature
Fully hardy

Harvesting period
Summer

Suitable container size
Min. 18in (45cm)

Suitable container material
Terra-cotta, glazed ceramic, stone

Medium type
Soil-based medium, eg, multipurpose potting soil

A warm, sunny, sheltered patio is the perfect site for this succulent, juicy fruit. Grow as a bush, or if you're tight for space, fan-train the tree on a framework of canes against a south- or west-facing wall or fence. Apricots are hardy, but because they flower early in the year the blossom and young buds are vulnerable to spring frosts—lose them and you won't get any fruit. If the temperature threatens to dip below zero, protect your tree by wrapping it in floating row cover or bringing it under cover. Some of the new varieties, bred in North America and France, flower later, reducing the risk of frost damage.

When the baby fruits are about the size of a fingernail, thin them if there is a very heavy crop, and then thin to a spacing of 2–4in (5–10cm). Water regularly, feed, and boost pollination as for peaches (*see opposite*). Net developing fruits to protect them from birds and squirrels. Despite all your efforts, though, it has to be said that a bumper crop is dependent on a long, hot summer.

ROOTSTOCK CHOICE
Like peaches, apricots are available on dwarfing rootstocks, including 'Saint Julien A' (*see opposite*). Trees suitable for container growing are also available on 'Torinel' rootstock, which is termed "semi-vigorous." They are slightly taller, but still manageable, and produce heavy crops.

Apricots, like peaches, need heat to ripen.

TENDER FRUIT

CHOOSING APRICOT VARIETIES

Flavorcot ('Boyoto') is a North American-bred variety that is a very heavy cropper. It produces large, orange-red fruits with a firm texture and intense flavor. Self-fertile.

'Petit Muscat' produces an abundance of walnut-sized, yellow and red fruits. The apricots are deliciously fragrant with an intense, juicy sweetness. Self-fertile.

'Tomcot' is the earliest cropping apricot. Its red-flushed fruits, which look pretty on the tree, are ready to pick in midsummer. It is self-fertile and a heavy cropper.

'Alfred' has large, oval-shaped fruits with attractive orange-blushed skins and juicy orange flesh. Trees are self-fertile and have good disease resistance.

Exotic fruits

It's surprising what you can grow in containers on a warm patio. If you love Mexican food you could be harvesting your own homegrown tomatilloes, which are a key ingredient in the classic salsa verde. Or, for the health-conscious, save a small fortune by growing your own "superfoods." High in antioxidants, the jewellike goji and aronia berries are easy to grow and make attractive plants.

Tomatillo

Plant used
Tomatillo 'Toma Verde'

Height and spread
H & S 3ft (1m)

Exposure
Full sun

Temperature
Not hardy below 32°F (0°C)

Harvesting period
Late summer

Suitable pot size
8in (20cm)

Suitable container material
Plastic

Medium type
Soil-based medium, eg, multipurpose potting soil

Related to the Cape gooseberry, tomatilloes have plump fruit hidden inside a papery husk, only in this case they are green. These vigorous, tender plants produce masses of large, yellow flowers, followed in late summer by the fruits, which are the essential ingredient in green salsas in Mexican cooking.

STARTING FROM SEED
Sow seed thinly in small pots in late winter and early spring, transplanting the seedlings into individual pots when they are big enough to handle. Plants can go outdoors in a warm, sunny, sheltered area after the last frost. In cool summer areas, they will crop better in a sunroom or greenhouse. Like their cousin the tomato, they like to be planted as deeply as possible. Tomatilloes aren't self-fertile, so you will need more than one for pollination.

Like indeterminate tomatoes (also a relation), the stems of tomatilloes need to be tied to canes to support the weight of the fruits. Don't overwater or you'll ruin their flavor, and feed occasionally with a balanced liquid fertilizer.

> **TOP TIP: HARVESTING**
>
> Havest tomatilloes in later summer, when the husks dry out completely and split away from the fruit, which will be about the size of a golf ball and are still green. Remove the husks and discard.

Tomatilloes are related to Cape gooseberries and tomatoes and look like it too with their green papery husk surrounding the fruit that looks just like a small green tomato.

TENDER FRUIT

Goji berry

Plant used
Goji berry

Height and spread
H & S 4ft (1.2m)

Exposure
Sun or partial shade

Temperature
Fully hardy

Harvesting period
Fall

Suitable pot size
12in (30cm)

Suitable container material
Terra-cotta, stone, glazed ceramic

Medium type
Soil-based medium, eg, John Innes No 3, with extra grit

The red, oval fruits of the goji or wolfberry are displayed like jewels on the branches of this hardy shrub. As well as their aesthetic appeal, the berries are also crammed with antioxidants, vitamins, and minerals. Young goji plants are available in spring, ready to plant out into 12in (30cm) pots of soil-based medium. To improve drainage, add extra grit to the medium and raise the containers on "feet," and boost plant growth by mixing a slow-release, balanced fertilizer into the medium. Water regularly year-round, and lightly prune the plants in spring. The goji produces purple or pink flowers in summer, which are subsequently followed by the brightly colored autumn fruits. Remember, however, that plants won't crop until their second year. Shake berries from the branches rather than picking them off.

TOP TIP: DRYING BERRIES

Berries can be used fresh or dried. To dry them, spread the fruits in a single layer on a wire rack and allow to dry naturally in a warm and light place. Alternatively, dry the berries on a rack in an oven set on a low temperature. Avoid touching the fruits as their skins will discolor your hands.

Aronia berry

Plant used
Aronia berry

Height and spread
H & S 4ft (1.2m)

Exposure
Sun or partial shade

Temperature
Fully hardy

Harvesting period
Fall

Suitable pot size
12in (30cm)

Suitable container material
Terra-cotta, stone, glazed ceramic

Medium type
Soil-based medium, eg, multipurpose potting soil

The nutrient-rich, black currant-like berries of aronia or chokeberries can be juiced or made into jam. In spring and summer, this deciduous shrub forms a mound of glossy green foliage, but in fall the leaves turn a fiery red, which is even brighter if plants are placed in full sun. The small, white, spring flowers are followed by dark purple autumn berries.

In their native habitat, aronias are found growing in damp, acidic soil, but they will thrive in a range of soil conditions. Plant in pots of soil-based medium, such as John Innes No 3, and keep plants well watered.

WHAT TO GROW

The wild species of aronia produce prolific crops of berries, but more compact cultivars, such as Iroquois Beauty ('Morton') and 'Hugin', are better suited to the cramped conditions in a container.

Aronia berries contain high levels of vitamins and antioxidants and although a tree might not produce much fruit during the first couple of years, after that it should yield a great many more. They are self-fertile.

Lemons and limes

Sweetly fragrant flowers, followed by delicious, aromatic fruits make lemon and lime trees highly desirable plants for a cool sunroom in winter, and a warm, sheltered patio throughout summer. Both trees are easy to grow if you can provide the right conditions, and your rewards will be juicy fruits and elegant plants to dress up your home.

TENDER FRUIT

Lemons

Plant used
Citrus x *meyeri* 'Meyer'

Height and spread
H 6ft (1.8m)
S 5ft (1.5m)

Exposure
Bright and sunny

Temperature needs
Min. 45°F (7°C)

Harvesting period
Varies, depending on type

Suitable pot size
18in (45cm)

Suitable container material
Terra-cotta, stone, glazed ceramic

Medium type
Specialty citrus medium

Growing your own lemon tree will instantly transport you to the groves of Italy or California, where the scent of these highly fragrant fruits hangs heavy in the air. There are many good varieties to choose from. *Citrus limon* 'Variegata' has two-tone green and yellow leaves and stripy fruit, while 'Meyer' is a compact variety that produces heavy crops of rounded fruit. Ideal for a light, bright, frost-free sunroom or greenhouse, lemons can be moved outside in summer to a warm, sunny patio or terrace.

OVERWINTERING LEMONS
Plant in large pots of specialized citrus medium, water regularly with rainwater, and feed monthly in summer with a fertilizer formulated for citrus fruits. Lemons, like all citrus, are frost-tender plants and may suffer at temperatures below 45°F (7°C). However, they can also fail to fruit if they are too warm in winter, so try to maintain a temperature of 50–59°F (10–15°C). Reduce watering and feed less frequently in winter with a specialized winter citrus fertilizer.

Lemons grow happily outside in summer when given plenty of water. Ensure the root ball is completely soaked.

TOP TIP: PLANTING SEEDS

Although it's easier to buy a plant (and it will fruit well), it's also fun to try growing your own lemon tree from a seed. Sow seeds from ripe fruit, ½in (1cm) deep, in small pots filled with seed medium. Place in a heated propagator. Seedlings appear quite quickly but fruit-bearing trees take many years to grow.

Limes

Plant used
Lime

Height and spread
H 6ft (1.8m)
S 5ft (1.5m)

Exposure
Bright

Temperature needs
Min. 45°F (7°C)

Harvesting period
Summer, but can be
year-round

Suitable pot size
18in (45cm)

**Suitable container
material**
Terra-cotta, stone,
glazed ceramic

Medium type
Specialty citrus
medium

If you would like homegrown limes to add to your drinks or Asian or Mexican dishes, you can keep a tree in a large container in a light, bright, sunny area, such as a heated greenhouse or cool sunroom. Before considering a lime, make sure that you will have space to move around the plant, as its stems are armed with vicious spines. Grow and overwinter limes as you would lemon trees (*see opposite*), and water plants regularly, allowing the medium to almost dry out before applying more.

HARVESTING LIMES
It's difficult to know when fruits are ripe just by looking at them, as they don't change color. However, the fruits do turn a lighter green when they are ready. The skins also feel smooth, and fruits are slightly soft when gently squeezed. To remove, twist the limes carefully from the plant.

Lime trees are armed with sharp spines.

Makrut limes

Plant used
Makrut lime

Height and spread
H 6ft (1.8m)
S 5ft (1.5m)

Exposure
Bright

Temperature needs
Min. 45°F (7°C)

Harvesting period
Year-round for
leaves

Suitable pot size
18in (45cm)

**Suitable container
material**
Terra-cotta, plastic,
glazed ceramic

Medium type
Specialty citrus
medium

While most limes are grown for their fruit, the makrut lime (formerly known as kaffir lime) is mainly grown for its shiny green leaves, which are widely used as a flavoring in Thai cuisine. Apart from providing you with an ingredient that can be difficult to find in all but specialized food shops, the makrut lime is a handsome plant for a large pot. Young shoots are a bronze color, while each leaf is elongated and comprises two segments. Watch the stems, though, as they are armed with long spines.

GROWING LIMES
Plant up pots as for lemons (*see opposite*) and keep plants in a light sunroom or greenhouse. Ensure that temperatures do not fall below 45°F (7°C) at night and that they are a little higher during the day in winter, although they will enjoy hotter conditions in summer. Limes respond to sudden changes in temperature by dropping their leaves, but can recover when acclimatized. Feed, water, and overwinter the same as for lemons.

Makrut lime leaves and fruits.

Hothouse fruit

You can create your own mini orangery, or grow other citrus fruits, such as mandarins, tangerines, and the weird and wonderful Buddha's hand, if you have a frost-free greenhouse or sunroom. Provide trees with sufficient light and heat, and you can produce a range of jewellike fruits.

TENDER FRUIT

Plant used
Calamondin orange

Height and spread
Standard tree:
H 5ft (1.5m)
S 3ft (1m)

Exposure
Bright indoors; full sun outside

Temperature needs
Not hardy below 32°F (0°C); min. 57°F (14°C) when fruiting

Harvesting period
Summer to fall

Suitable pot size
18in (45cm)

Suitable container material
Terra-cotta, stone, glazed ceramic, plastic

Medium type
Specialty citrus medium or soil-based medium, eg, John Innes No 3, with extra grit

Living in a cool climate, it is hard to imagine plucking citrus fruits from the branches of your own tree, but it is quite possible in the warmth of a heated greenhouse or sunroom.

Plants are widely available from specialized nurseries, most of which offer mail-order services. The trees require large, sturdy containers filled with specialty citrus or soil-based medium, and a bright position, as they will perform badly in poor light. They can be placed outside during the summer months, but ensure plants are moved back indoors before nighttime temperatures start to fall at the end of summer or beginning of fall.

CARING FOR CITRUS PLANTS

Plants need regular watering, especially when the fruits are developing because dry medium at this stage can cause them to drop prematurely. Citrus trees do not like hard, calcium-rich water, so try to use rainwater if possible, and feed every month in spring and summer with a special liquid fertilizer formulated for citrus plants in active growth. Reduce watering and feeding in winter—when you do water, add a half-strength solution of fertilizer designed for citrus plants in winter.

To fruit well, citrus plants need a temperature of at least 57°F (14°C) for the six months after flowering, and they may become dormant if temperatures fall below this. It can also take up to 11 months for fruit to ripen after the flowers have been pollinated.

*Center: **Calamondin is a dwarf orange** that produces sweet fruits and can tolerate lower temperatures than many citruses.*

TOP TIP: PRUNING CITRUS TREES

Citrus plants do not require any major pruning. Simply remove any dead, diseased, or damaged branches as you notice them, along with any crossing stems that may rub and create wounds. Then reduce the sideshoots to maintain an attractive rounded shape. Pruning is best carried out between winter and early spring.

Citrus tree choices

Orange trees are widely available and some are hardy to 23°F (-5°C). They have dark green, glossy leaves and white, scented flowers, followed by fruits in late spring and early summer. Choose a compact form for a pot. If you are looking for a more dramatic citrus tree, consider Citrus medica var. digitata, known as Buddha's hand. With its large and inedible fingerlike fruits, this is one of the most surprising fruits you are ever likely to see. The plants need heat to thrive.

TENDER FRUIT

Mandarin trees often bear fruits from spring until fall. There are many cultivars to choose from, with plants in a range of sizes and fruits with different flavors. The branches are quite brittle and may need supporting.

Kumquat is a slow-growing tree that produces orange, egg-shaped fruits with a sweet skin and slightly bitter flesh. Fruits are ready to harvest between late fall and midwinter, and follow white, scented flowers.

Tangerine trees are part of the mandarin family and produce small, sweet, easy-to-peel fruits. Look out for tangelo plants, too, which are crosses between tangerines and grapefruits or oranges.

Clementine trees are often sold as standards with bushy heads of dark, evergreen leaves. Grown for their small, sweet fruits, clementines can be harvested between fall and midwinter, depending on the variety.

Fruit medley

These three fascinating fruits will tantalize your taste buds and are guaranteed to create a talking point. Pineapples and guavas are fun to grow but both are tropical fruits and need the protection of a warm, bright sunroom, while quinces make striking specimens for outdoor containers, and the fruits are prized ingredients for pickles and jellies.

Pineapple *Ananas comosus*

EXOTIC FRUITS

Plant used
Ananas comosus

Height and spread
H & S 3ft (1m)

Exposure
Full sun, in a warm, bright sunroom

Temperature
Min. 59°F (15°C)

Harvesting period
When fruit is fully ripened

Suitable pot size
8in (20cm)

Suitable container material
Plastic, place inside a decorative pot holder

Medium type
Soil-based medium, eg, John Innes No 3 with added grit

A member of the tropical bromeliad family, the pineapple is an attractive plant with strappy, spiny leaves and spiky-topped fruit. For something so exotic, pineapples are surprisingly easy to grow. Either buy ready-grown plants or start your own in spring from store-bought fruit. Cut a thick slice off the top of the pineapple and remove the lower leaves. Scoop out any soft flesh and leave this to dry for a few days before planting, scoop-side down, in a pot of soil-based medium.

A warm, bright sunroom is essential for growing pineapples as they need six hours of bright sun a day and a minimum temperature of 64°F (18°C). Water regularly, especially when the plant is young, and put a thick organic mulch (*see p.58*) on the surface of the container to help retain moisture. Each plant will produce a single fruit. To harvest them, wait for them to turn yellow, then cut through the stem below each fruit, leaving a small stalk attached.

TOP TIP: ENCOURAGING FRUITING

Pineapples grow slowly and won't fruit until they are at least three years old. They need a bright, sunny spot. Keep the "well" between the leaf rosettes full of water, and mist plants now and then. When in growth, feed once a month with a liquid tomato fertilizer.

Tropical pineapples make striking architectural focal points for a bright south-facing sunroom, where the bright light and warmth will suit their needs to perfection.

Guava *Psidium guajava*

Plant used
Psidium guajava

Height and spread
H & S 8ft (2m)

Exposure
Full sun

Temperature
Min. 37°F (3°C)

Harvesting period
Late spring

Suitable pot size
12in (30cm) or larger

Suitable container material
Terra-cotta, stone, glazed ceramic

Medium type
Soil-based medium, eg, multipurpose potting soil

Small, green guava fruit is rarely seen in markets, and plants will be the star attraction when grown in a sunroom in cooler climates. They can be grown from seed, but it's easier to start with a young plant. Guavas need plenty of space and lots of light, so plant them in large containers filled with soil-based medium and set in a warm, bright sunroom. Trees can go outside in summer in a sheltered area next to a warm, south-facing wall, but both the early blossom and ripening fruits must be protected from frost. Plants will only fruit after a long, hot summer.

CARING FOR YOUR TREES

Ensure the medium doesn't dry out, but avoid overwatering. Give guavas a boost in spring by working a slow-release, balanced fertilizer into the top layer of medium. Keep plants bushy and within bounds by pruning shoot tips in spring.

Guavas have a sweet, pineapple-mint flavor.

Quince *Cydonia oblonga*

Plant used
Cydonia oblonga

Height and spread
Standard plants:
H 5ft (1.5m)
S 3ft (1m)

Exposure
Full sun

Temperature
Hardy, but avoid frost pockets

Harvesting period
Fall

Suitable pot size
Min. 18in (45cm)

Suitable container material
Terra-cotta, stone

Medium type
Soil-based medium, eg, multipurpose potting soil

Quince fruits are aromatic as well as ornamental.

The aromatic, pear-shaped, yellow fruits of *Cydonia* are used to make a sweet jelly to serve with meats and cheese, and are a world away from the far less palatable fruits that appear on the ornamental Japanese quince (*Chaenomeles*).

Grow trees in large containers of soil-based medium and stand in the sunniest, warmest spot possible outside to ensure the fruits ripen. Keep plants well watered and raise containers on "feet" to aid drainage. In late winter, remove the top layer of medium in the pot and replace with fresh, mixed with a slow-release, balanced granular fertilizer. Quinces can become quite large, but standard plants are more compact. Pruning the shoot tips also limits their sprawl.

HARVESTING FRUIT

Fruits are ready to harvest when they turn golden in late fall. Pick before they get hit by frost. Store quinces, unwrapped, in a cool, dry, dark place and, because they are highly scented, store them separately from other fruits.

PROBLEM SOLVER

Pests and diseases in the garden are a fact of life, but damage can be limited by creating barriers and encouraging beneficial wildlife. Feeding and watering your crops pay dividends too. If the worst should happen, and you find spots on your apples or holes in your zucchini, the troubleshooting guide in this section will help you deal with the main pests and diseases you might encounter.

Help your plants remain strong and healthy by using copper tape to keep slugs at bay, encouraging beneficial insects into your garden, and using water to help destroy aphids.

Keeping pests and diseases at bay

The risk to plants from pests and diseases can be reduced by growing them in the conditions they enjoy, and checking them at regular intervals so that you are able to deal with any problems as they arise. In addition, where a plant is particularly prone to a disease, choose a resistant variety and then grow them in as healthy a way as possible.

Reduce the risks

Healthy plants will often shrug off attacks from pests and diseases, so ensure yours are not under stress by growing them in appropriate conditions and watering regularly. Feed plants according to their needs, but avoid overfeeding, as aphids love the resulting soft growth.

Keeping pots free of plant debris and weeds is also good practice, leaving pests and diseases with nowhere to hide or overwinter, so tidy the area you're cultivating regularly. Also inspect your plants regularly for signs of attack. Shriveled or distorted leaves and shoots are often a sign of aphid infestation, while holes in leaves may be due to slugs, snails, or caterpillars. Check flower buds and the undersides of leaves, and either pick off the culprits, in the case of slugs and snails, or, wearing gardening gloves, wipe off aphids or use a spray hose to wash them off. Simply squashing greenfly or small caterpillars can be remarkably effective. Prevent diseases by sterilizing pots and tools (*see pp.32–33*) when growing seeds, and pick off and discard any infected leaves, flowers, or stems.

Drought-stressed plants grow below par and are at risk from pest attacks. Keeping plants well watered will help prevent problems; for hanging baskets this can mean twice a day in the height of summer.

TOP TIP: WEEDING

Do all you can to remove weeds from your containers, as they will compete with your crops for water, space, and nutrition, and may also harbor pests and diseases. Try to remove them before weeds have a chance to flower and produce more seeds. If possible, weed on a dry day. Dig out perennial weeds with a hand fork, and try to ensure that you remove the entire root.

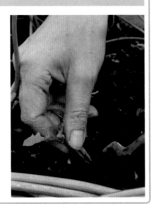

Choose healthy plants

To ensure that pests and diseases are not unwittingly brought into your garden, check plants carefully before you buy them. Reject any that are wilting, have yellow or marked foliage, or have weeds growing on the medium surface that may be carrying diseases.

In addition, where possible, select disease-resistant plants. You will find many that offer resistance to infection as you scan through catalogs and read plant labels. Many new selections of tomatoes and other vegetables also provide resistance to viruses and blight.

An easy way to spot exceptional plants is to look for plants with a recoginized seal of quality. Plants that receive accolades are often recommended as "tried-and-tested" choices.

Above: **Healthy plants** *at a garden center will look cared for, have no browning leaves, and will be growing in fresh medium with no weeds.*

Use physical barriers

Barriers are a very useful way of preventing pests from getting to your prized crops, let alone damaging them. Most are designed to counteract the pest by being uncomfortable to cross or impossible to jump or climb over. Copper tape and bands of petroleum jelly or grease make movement difficult for slimy creatures.

Take care to remove fallen vegetation around your containers as this can create a bridge that will soon be discovered and exploited to the full. Sharp grit, gravel, and ground-up eggshells are used relatively successfully to restrict snail damage. Used on their own, each provides a modicum of protection, but if they are used in conjunction with biological control, and safe and responsible use of slug pellets (which are toxic), any damage will be minimal.

Above: **Wrap a strip** *of copper tape around containers to ward off slugs and snails. It is supposed to give them a small but harmless electric shock.*

Left: **Net strawberries** *and other fruit to guard against birds. Nets may not be the most attractive addition to your patio, but they are invaluable.*

Organic pest control

Every garden, no matter how well tended, will have its share of pests and diseases to contend with. When you are growing your own food, you may prefer not to spray crops with pesticides. Instead, try for natural biological control by encouraging, or introducing, populations of beneficial creatures to prey on persistent pests.

Encourage pest predators

Providing food, water, and shelter for a wide range of wildlife will encourage them into your garden, where they will feed on pests and help keep their numbers under control. Feeders will bring in birds that also have a taste for aphids, caterpillars, snails, and other pests.

Growing flowers among your crops not only adds color, but also encourages pollinating insects to visit. These often feed on pests, too. The scent of flowers may also prevent pests locating crops.

Where an insect pest does take hold, it is possible to introduce a biological control, such as beneficial nematodes, to combat them. Microscopic, parasitic nematode worms effectively control a range of pests, including slugs, snails, caterpillars, and weevils. They come in a paste, which is watered into the soil using a watering can.

Golden French marigolds not only mix well with tomatoes, thyme, and basil, they are also relatively pest free and attract beneficial insects, such as lacewings, ladybugs, and parasitic wasps.

Create habitats

Creating different habitats entices all kinds of beneficial creatures to take up residence. A pond will bring frogs, toads, and insects, as well as other hungry and thirsty animals and birds. Similarly, hiding places, such as piles of leaves, pieces of old carpet, or propped-up slates, provide shelter for helpful creatures such as toads and frogs. A log pile provides a home for beetles and frogs, too, and can even make a winter shelter for a snake. Leave a few piles undisturbed in nooks of the garden to tempt in these beneficial creatures. If you find pests such as snails sheltering, too, just remove them.

Use a half barrel to make a pond and attract all manner of useful creatures to your garden. Position the barrel in a sunny spot, add a pond liner, and then fill it with water and a host of small aquatic plants and fish.

BENEFICIAL BUGS

Many insects pollinate crops and some feed voraciously on common insect pests, so it's a good idea to make your garden attractive to them.

Lacewing larvae and adults feast on aphids and other insect pests. Attract them into your garden with nectar-rich flowers.

Ladybug adults and larvae have a voracious appetite for aphids and will actively seek out infested plants. Provide dry places, such as seedheads, for them to overwinter.

Hoverflies are larvae that devour aphids and the adults pollinate crops. Encourage them with colorful flowers.

Centipedes have an eager appetite for all kinds of soil pests and are at home in leaf litter and log piles.

Frogs and toads eat slugs and insects, and will visit your garden if you have a small pond or pool.

A pond attracts frogs and toads, which will result in fewer slugs in your garden.

Ladybugs enthusiastically dine on aphids. Encourage them to stay over winter by leaving some seedheads on plants.

Common pests

Most plants in the kitchen garden are prone to attack by many different insect and animal pests. Healthy crops often cope well with attacks, but stay vigilant and check for pests regularly, as some can multiply quickly, resulting in seriously harmed plants and reduced harvests.

1 APHIDS
Aphids include greenfly and blackfly and are found on young shoots of most plants. They distort growth and transmit viruses. Squash them, encourage natural predators, or use pyrethrum or insecticidal soap sprays.

2 CODLING MOTH
Larvae bore into apples and pears in summer. Use a biological control in fall or use an insecticide labeled for codling moth in early summer.

3 ASPARAGUS BEETLE
Adult beetles and their larvae feed on asparagus foliage and gnaw the stems in late spring and summer, causing stems to die back. Pick off the pest, spray with an appropriate insecticide, and burn cut stems in fall.

4 FLEA BEETLE
These tiny black beetles pepper the leaves of brassicas and allied plants, such as rutabaga and radishes, with countless little holes, damaging

seedlings and spoiling salad leaves, such as arugula. Grow your brassica crops under row cover or surround affected areas with a strip of bare ground to eliminate hiding places.

5 CAPSID BUGS
These tiny insects suck sap from many plants, causing brown-edged holes in leaves and deformed fruits. Control is usually unnecessary, but apples can be sprayed with an appropriate insecticide after flowering.

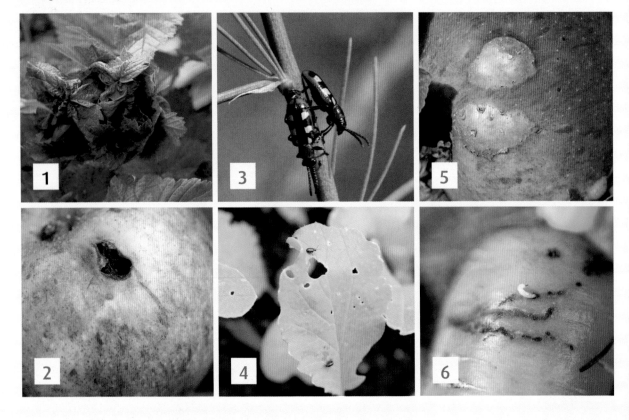

6 CARROT RUST FLY

The thin, creamy maggots of this small fly tunnel into carrots and parsnips. No insecticide is effective, so grow resistant crop varieties and cover your seedlings with row cover.

7 CABBAGE CATERPILLARS

Several butterfly and moth species lay eggs on brassicas, which then hatch into leaf-eating caterpillars. Pick off eggs and caterpillars, and cover with fine netting.

8 BIRD DAMAGE

Hungry birds feed on seeds, buds, fruit, and foliage. Soft fruit and brassicas are especially favorite targets. Cover vulnerable beds and bushes with netting, well secured at the base, to prevent birds getting in and becoming trapped.

9 BEET LEAF MINER

The leaves of beets, Swiss chard, and spinach beet are mined by the maggots of these flies. The affected areas of the leaves turn white or pale green, then they go brown and dry up. Two generations occur: one in early summer and a second in late summer. This pest is difficult to control with insecticides, so pick off infested leaves or grow the plants under floating row cover.

10 GOOSEBERRY SAWFLY

The green, black-spotted larvae of this sawfly have seven pairs of clasping legs and can quickly devour the leaves of gooseberries and red currants in spring and summer, causing severe damage. Pick them off by hand or use a biological control.

11 LEEK MOTH

The young caterpillars create pale brown patches on onion and leek foliage by mining the leaves, while more mature caterpillars bore into the flesh of the vegetables. Grow leeks and onions under floating row cover to exclude the moth.

12 CURRANT APHID

Leaves at the shoot tips on red, white, and black currants develop reddish or yellowish green blisters in spring. The currant blister aphid has little impact on the fruit, so control is not necessary.

CATS (not illustrated)

Cats love digging in soft seedbeds and they may also tear protective netting and floating row cover. Use chicken wire to keep them off.

13 MICE

Pea and bean seeds in the soil and stored fruits and vegetables are all irresistible to these rodents. They are difficult to control, but you can set traps where they are a problem.

14 WASPS

Wasps prey on other insects in early summer, but they eat ripe fruit, especially plums, grapes, and apples, as the season progresses. Distract them with wasp traps or damaged ripe fruit placed away from trees.

15 PEA MOTH

Adult moths fly in midsummer, laying their eggs on peas in flower. Caterpillars hatch and grow inside the pods, eating the peas. Early and late sowings avoid the egg-laying adults, but summer crops should be netted.

16 APPLE LEAF MINER

The tiny caterpillars feed inside the leaves of apples and cherries, creating long, narrow, twisting white or brown lines on the upper leaf surface. Several generations occur during the summer, but heavy infestations are generally not seen before late summer. By then, it is too late for the pest to damage the tree, so control measures are not required.

17 AMERICAN RASPBERRY BEETLE

The slender brownish white grubs of this pest damage the fruits of raspberries, blackberries, and their hybrids. They feed at the stalk end of the berries, causing dry, gray-brown patches. Control the American raspberry beetle by hanging out white sticky traps to catch adults as they feed.

18 PLUM FRUIT MOTH

Pale pink, brown-headed caterpillars feed near the stones of greengages, plums, and damsons. Hang up pheromone traps in June, to trap adult males and disrupt mating.

19 RED SPIDER MITE

Glasshouse and fruit tree red spider mites both cause dull, mottled leaves on a range of plants. Keep glasshouse humidity high in hot weather and use a biological control. Try insecticidal soap spray or plant oil sprays outdoors, as directed on the package.

20 WOOLLY APHIDS

This pest sucks sap from the woody stems of apple trees, secreting fluffy white waxy material between spring and early fall. Scrub off with a stiff brush in spring to early summer.

21 SLUGS AND SNAILS
These slimy pests eat holes in leaves and roots, and can rapidly destroy rows of seedlings. Limit numbers by collecting at night or in traps, or scatter wood ash around plantings. In summer, biological control is effective.

22 PEA AND BEAN WEEVIL
Little gray-brown beetles that nibble notches from leaf edges. The larvae feed among the roots of peas. Large plants tolerate damage, but it may be better to raise young plants in pots.

23 WHITEFLY
White-winged, sap-feeding insects that excrete sticky honeydew, whitefly are usually at their worst on greenhouse crops, such as tomatoes and cucumbers. Control with *Encarsia formosa*, a parasitic wasp, is effective.

24 WIREWORMS
Larvae of click beetles, these slim, orange-brown larvae live in the soil, biting through seedlings and damaging root crops, such as potatoes and carrots. Remove any visible larvae and dig up root crops promptly when they are ready to be harvested.

CABBAGE ROOT FLY *(not illustrated)*
From spring to fall these white larvae feed on brassica roots, and damage seedlings. Cover crops with fine mesh from mid- to late summer to prevent females from laying eggs at plant bases.

ROOT APHIDS *(not illustrated)*
Crops attract white aphids that suck sap from roots, affecting growth and causing wilting in hot weather. Water well during summer.

CUTWORMS *(not illustrated)*
Not, in fact, worms but the caterpillars of several moth species, cutworms chew through the topmost roots of young plants or make holes in root vegetables. Handpick the pale brown caterpillars from the soil around wilting plants, wrap paper or foil tubes around seedlings to exclude cutworms.

PEAR MIDGE *(not illustrated)*
Signs of pear midge are pear fruitlets turning black at the eye and stop growing, and drop in early summer. The maggots hatch from eggs laid in blossom and they feed in the fruitlets. Remove and destroy affected fruitlets to control pest numbers in the future.

For general advice on organic pest control, *see pp.174–175.*

19 21 23 20 22 24

Common diseases and disorders

It can seem like there's an army of bacteria, fungi, and viruses out there all waiting to thwart your attempts to grow your own produce. Fortunately, healthy plants are more likely to resist disease, so tend them well, keep the garden tidy to reduce sources of infection, and rotate crops to prevent disease building up.

1 CANKER

Many fruit trees are affected by cankers. Shoots die back and sunken bark may ooze resin. Prune back to healthy growth or treat with copper fungicides as directed on the label.

2 HONEY FUNGUS

Fruit trees and bushes can be killed by honey fungus, which causes die-back. Destroy plants with white fungal growth and a mushroom smell under the bark at the base.

3 BITTER PIT *(disorder)*

Dark spots or pits appear on the skin of developing apples, and fruit may taste bitter due to drought-induced calcium deficiency. Mulch apple trees and water well in dry weather.

4 CHOCOLATE SPOT

Dark brown spots appear on foliage and stems, reducing or destroying the crop. The fungus flourishes in damp conditions, so grow plants widely spaced and on well-drained soil.

5 BOTRYTIS

This fungus infects plants growing under glass, lettuce, and soft fruit. It causes a fuzzy gray mold, rotting, and die-back. Remove infected growth and ventilate greenhouses.

6 BROWN ROT

A widespread fungus that infects tree fruit, causing rotten patches and creamy pustules. Remove infected fruit promptly, along with branches affected by blossom wilt (*see p.182*).

7 AMERICAN GOOSEBERRY MILDEW

Powdery white patches develop on leaves and young shoots, causing dead leaves and stunted shoots. Gooseberry fruits are also badly affected. Prune infected tissue to encourage good airflow, and use a fungicide labeled for this use, but avoid excessive use of nitrogenous fertilizers. Keep watered and mulched in dry periods. Resistant varieties are available.

8 BLOSSOM END ROT (disorder)

This appears as dark patches at the base of tomatoes, peppers, and other fruit. It occurs because of calcium deficiency (see p.185), which is usually caused by drought conditions. Water the plants consistently to protect developing crops from contracting this disease.

9 CLUB ROOT

This fungal infection produces enlarged, distorted roots on brassica plants, causing wilting, purple-tinged foliage, and possibly die-back. Grow resistant varieties. Reducing soil acidity by liming may also help.

10 CUCUMBER MOSAIC VIRUS

Aphids carry the virus between cucumbers and related crops, such as zucchini. Leaves pucker and yellow, and fruit distorts and is inedible. Remove and burn infected plants.

11 DAMPING OFF

The disease causes seedlings to collapse suddenly. To reduce the risk, which is caused by fungi, use clean pots and tap water. Sow plants thinly, provide good ventilation, and apply a copper-based fungicide.

12 DOWNY MILDEW

Thriving in humid conditions, this fungus causes brown patches on upper leaves, with fluffy growth beneath. Brassicas, lettuce, and other plants are affected. Destroy diseased leaves and give plants ample space.

BACTERIAL SOFT ROT (not illustrated)

This causes sunken, rotten areas on the roots and fruits of crops, such as brassicas, potatoes, tomatoes, and zucchini. The infection is spread by insects or dirty tools. The bacteria enter through wounds so can be spread on pruning tools and insects.

POTATO BLACK LEG (not illustrated)

Yellowing foliage, as early as June, and black areas at stem bases are signs of this bacterial disease. Destroy infected plants and rotate crops.

13 FUNGAL LEAF SPOT

Circular gray or brown spots on leaves, sometimes with tiny black fruiting bodies, are caused by fungi on many types of crops, from strawberries to celery. This is not usually serious, but remove affected leaves to prevent the fungus spreading further.

14 BLOSSOM WILT

Many fruit trees suffer from this disease, which is worse in damp springs. Usually the flowers wilt and turn brown, and the fungus that causes blossom wilt may grow into the spur to kill leaves or form cankers on branches. Spores are blown from overwintering infections to attack the flowers as they open. Remove affected flowers, wood, and fruit promptly to prevent spread.

15 ROOT ROT

Common in greenhouse-grown cucumbers and tomatoes, these fungal rots set in at the base of the stem, killing the whole plant. Remove and destroy infected plants, and practice good garden hygiene.

16 ONION WHITE ROT

Signs that this fungus has attacked the bulbs of onions, leeks, and garlic are white, dense, slightly fluffy fungal growth and yellowing and wilting foliage. It persists in soil for years, so don't spread contaminated soil.

17 FIREBLIGHT

A bacterial disease of apples and pears. Leaves of affected branches wilt and brown, and it can spread down the inner bark. Prune out and burn infected branches promptly.

18 PEACH LEAF CURL

Red or pale green blisters develop on new leaves, which swell and curl, and are later covered in white spores. Apply a copper fungicide as buds begin to swell in midwinter and two weeks later. Remove diseased tissue.

19 POTATO BLIGHT

A problem in warm, wet summers, this fungus affects potatoes and tomatoes (*see p.184*), causing foliage to rot and tubers to be infected. Destroy infected foliage, lift tubers early, and grow resistant varieties.

20 POTATO COMMON SCAB

Potato scab causes raised brown patches on the skin of potatoes. It is worse on dry and alkaline soils, so water well, avoid liming before they crop, and choose resistant varieties.

21 POWDERY MILDEW
Many crops, including peas and currants, catch this fungus, which causes a white dusty layer on foliage. It is worse in dry conditions, so water well, remove fallen leaves, and use a fungicide as directed on the label.

22 RASPBERRY CANE SPOT
The white-centered purple spots caused by this fungus appear on canes and leaves of raspberries and hybrid berries, sometimes killing them. Burn affected canes.

23 RUST
Beans, leeks, pears, and plums are among crops that are infected by fungal rusts. Signs to be aware of include orange pustules on leaves and stems. Destroy infected material at harvest, and try to rotate crops.

24 SCAB
Apples and pears develop small, dark brown patches on their skin, which can spread to leaves and branches. The fungi responsible overwinter on fallen leaves, so tidy up detritus in the fall. Grow scab-resistant varieties.

BLACK CURRANT REVERSION VIRUS (not illustrated)
The virus, spread by mites, causes abnormally swollen buds and stunted growth. Burn infected plants and buy certified disease-free stock.

WHITE BLISTER (not illustrated)
This fungus produces shiny, white pustules on the undersides of brassica leaves, sometimes distorting them. Remove infected leaves or badly affected plants. Rotate crops and grow resistant varieties.

STRAWBERRY VIRUSES (not illustrated)
Strawberries are susceptible to a number of viral infections that are spread by insects or by pests in the soil, such as eelworms (nematodes). The viral symptoms include yellow-blotched or crumpled leaves and poor growth. Dig up and destroy infected plants and rotate your crops to prevent further recurrences.

ONION NECK ROT (not illustrated)
This fungal rot often affects onions, shallots, and garlic in storage, causing softening of the bulb and fuzzy gray mold. To prevent it spreading, check your stores regularly and promptly dispose of any infected bulbs. Don't grow onions, or related crops, in the same container year after year.

25 PLANT VIRUSES

Virus particles are invisible, even with the aid of a normal microscope, but the symptoms they cause are easily visible. Most commonly these appear as yellow leaf markings and leaf distortion, often accompanied by general poor growth and stunting. They are found throughout an infected plant, but symptoms may only be apparent on one area. Destroy infected plants and sterilize tools.

26 SCORCH *(disorder)*

Hot sun and cold dry winds can both scorch leaves and flowers, turning them brown and crisp. Sun scorch is especially damaging if there are water droplets on the plants. Avoid watering at the hottest times of day and ensure that greenhouse plants have adequate shading.

27 SILVER LEAF

Plums, cherries, apricots, and peaches are affected by this fungal disease. Leaves develop a silvery sheen, branches die back, and small purple bracket fungi may appear on dead wood. Infectious spores are produced in fall and winter. Cutting dying branches in the summer to below where staining ends can save the tree.

28 SHOTHOLE

Plums and cherries are affected by various fungal and bacterial infections, including bacterial canker and occasionally powdery mildews. In midsummer spots or blotches of discolored tissues develop. The areas then fall out, leaving holes. No insects are present. Destroy all infected and fallen leaves, spray dormant oil in winter.

29 TOMATO BLIGHT

Outdoor tomatoes are more susceptible to this fungal disease than those in the greenhouse. Watch for rapidly spreading wet rots on leaves and brown patches on fruit. Quickly remove and destroy infected material.

30 SCLEROTINA

This serious fungal disease affects lettuce, cucumbers, celery, tomatoes, and beans. Plants rapidly yellow and collapse with wet stem rot and fluffy white mold. Quickly remove and destroy diseased plants.

VIOLET ROOT ROT *(not illustrated)*

Root vegetables are damaged by this fungus. Usually found on wet, acid soils, it produces a mass of purple threads around roots, which then rot. Lift and burn infected plants.

Common nutrient deficiencies

Plants need a balanced intake of nutrients to remain healthy; mainly nitrogen, potassium (potash), and phosphorus, plus essential trace elements. Nutrients are often present in soil, but "locked up" if the pH is too high or low, or conditions are dry, so it pays to improve your soil and keep plants well fed.

1 BORON
Symptoms include splitting and discoloration of root vegetables and sweet corn due to limed or dry soils. Apply borax with clean, sharp sand.

2 CALCIUM
Bitter pit (*see p.180*) and blossom end rot of tomatoes (*see p.181*) are the most common signs. Calcium uptake is limited in dry and acidic conditions, so water consistently and add lime to acidic soils to raise the pH to 6.5.

3 IRON
Leaves of affected plants turn yellow between the veins and brown at the edges. Apply acidic mulches and use a chelated iron treatment.

4 MAGNESIUM
A common deficiency in acid soils, after heavy rains or use of high potash fertilizers. Older leaves yellow first, then they turn red, purple, or brown between the veins. Treat with Epsom salts as a foliar spray.

5 NITROGEN
Nitrogen washes out of soil easily and all plants, except peas and beans, can become deficient with yellow leaves and spindly growth. Dig in compost and add high nitrogen fertilizer.

6 POTASSIUM
Leaves tinged yellow or purple or tips appearing scorched around the edges with poor fruiting, suggest deficiency, especially in potatoes and tomatoes. Use potassium sulfate or tomato food.

Index

Acknowledgments

Dorling Kindersley would like to thank the following: Fiona Wild and Constance Novis for proofreading; Michele Clarke for the index.

The publisher would like to thank the following for their kind permission to reproduce their photographs:

(Key: b-below/bottom; c-centre; l-left; r-right)

Blackmoor Nurseries: 66t, 161cl, cr, br. **Dobies of Devon:** 87tc, 93tc, tr, 101 tl, 103bl, 159bcr. **DT Brown Seeds:** 163br. **Marshalls Seeds:** 101cb. **Sutton Seeds:** 77br, 101tc, 103bcl, 167tr. **Thompson & Morgan:** 90r, 114/115c, 119bcl, 153bcr. **Victoriana Nursery:** 4tl, 117bl, ctl, 143bl, 149tr, 159tcl.

Dorling Kindersley: Alan Buckingham: 4ac, 27br, 40t, 42t, 43br, bl, 48bl, 51, 60tl, 61tl, 62tl, l, 63tl, 64tl, bl, 65tl, 67tl, br, 68tl, 69br, 77tr, 82b, 92cb, 93br, cr, bcl, bcr, 95r, 106r, 113bl. 117tl, 134c, bl, 136br, 137c, 139bc, 142r, 158c, 167cl, 175l, 176bl, tc, tr, br, 177bl, tr, 179tr, 180c, tl, br, 181tl, cb, br, 182bl, bc, 183br, 185tc, bc, br.

All other images copyright **DK Images**

3 1901 05218 2948